Your Ticket to Law School

Getting In and Staying In

Books by Lawrence Graham

Your Ticket to Law School
Your Ticket to Medical or Dental School
Your Ticket to Business School
Conquering College Life
Ten Point Plan for College Acceptance
Jobs in the Real World

Your Ticket to Law School

Getting In and Staying In

by Lawrence Graham

Bantam Books
Toronto • New York • London • Sydney • Auckland

YOUR TICKET TO LAW SCHOOL: GETTING IN AND STAYING IN

A Bantam Book / March 1985

For information address: Bantam Books, Inc.

Library of Congress Cataloging in Publication Data

Graham, Lawrence.
Your ticket to law school.
Bibliography: p. 130
1. Law schools—United States—Admission. I. Title.
KF285.G73 1985 340'.07'1173 84-91009
ISBN 0-553-34144-8 (pbk.)

Published simultaneously in the United States and Canada

Bantam Books are published by Bantam Books, Inc. Its trademark, consisting of the words "Bantam Books" and the portrayal of a rooster, is Registered in the United States Patent and Trademark Office and in other countries. Marca Registrada. Bantam Books, Inc., 666 Fifth Avenue, New York, New York 10103.

PRINTED IN THE UNITED STATES OF AMERICA

0 0 9 8 7 6 5 4 3 2 1

To Betty and Richard
(and in memory of
Hazel and Sonny)

Contents

Acknowledgments

Like the writing of this book, getting into law school seemed, at first, to be an insurmountable task. But what got me through both was the advice and the assistance that I received from so many people.

I would like to thank all of those people who have contributed to this research and to my personal experiences as I finally got my very own ticket to law school. As always, I want to thank my parents, Betty and Richard, who never said they wanted a doctor-son or a lawyer-son—but somehow got both. I am thankful that my brother Richard has had confidence in me and that he and his dental school are just a few minutes away when I need an excuse to leave the campus. And of course, I thank my Uncle Searcy, who introduced me to my first Supreme Court judge.

So much thanks goes to my friend and literary agent Susan Zeckendorf, because she was the one who took a chance on a young author. Thanks also to my editors, Barbara Alpert and Jonathan Skipp, who saw a need for this book.

My appreciation goes to Dr. Mirian Gilbert and all my other pre-law and lawyer friends who gave me either personal advice or information for this book: John Rose, Heywood Burns, Lawrence Hamdan, Jordan Horvath, Cheryl Davis, Solomon Watson, Jerome Davis, Gary Jenkins, Susan Beckett, Floyd Abrams, Martin Oppenheimer, Bruce Bozeman, Drew Kastner, Damon Keith, Margaret Morton, William Thompson, Leslie Fagenson, Roy Oppenheim, Rod Plummer, Conna Weiner, Stacey Blaustein, Susan Curnick, Molly Geraghty, Marianne Michaels, and Stephen Pfleger.

Special thanks goes to Thomas Danziger, whom I first met somewhere between Scarsdale and Los Angeles, and who has since provided me with encouraging information on third-year law-school life.

And still more special thanks goes to my former Princeton classmate, David Caplan, who warned me about Harvard and who served as my first-year interviewee.

Introduction

Do You Really Want to Become a Lawyer?

Each person has his or her own reasons for wanting to become a lawyer. While some of us are attracted by the scholarly study of legal systems, more of us are wooed by the prestige and starting salaries of the graduating law student. Before you begin the lengthy application process, you had better be sure that the legal profession is something that you want for yourself—not for your parents and not because all your friends are applying.

It's not unusual for a college student to select law school as a means to postpone facing the problems of the real world. Many graduating students don't know which careers they wish to pursue, and others simply can't find a decent job. The answer for many of these people is to apply to law school.

What are the excuses these students give when someone asks them why they're planning on a legal education?

- Law school will give me three more years to decide what I want to do with my life.
- Law school is a respectable excuse for not taking a job.
- A law degree will probably help me in whatever I do.
- My parents will be satisfied if I apply.
- A law degree is a guarantee that I'll be financially successful.
- Many of my classmates are applying, so there must be some benefit.

If these are some of the reasons you use to convince yourself that law school is the place for you, then you might as well throw away the application. While there may be some truth in any of these rationales, none of them is going to get you through three years of long hours and occasional sleepless nights studying and writing technical legal briefs.

Although law school is not easy, it can be very rewarding if there is a valid reason behind your decision to attend. This book will tell you not only how to succeed in the application process, but also what to expect once you've gotten into law school and how to survive some of the challenges that will confront you there.

Your Ticket to Law School will explain which college courses and activities will both impress the law school admissions office and aid you in your future legal studies. It will help you decide where to apply to law school and then help you give your application the "hard sell." From supplying Law School Admission Test (LSAT) strategies to offering ways of collecting the best recommendation letters, this guide will teach you the shortcuts and secrets that will help you get into the law school of your choice.

Along with suggestions on where to find financial aid and what to do after being accepted or rejected are aggressive admissions strategies provided by the author, who only one year ago got into every law school to which he applied. Also in this book are interviews and information on life during the first year of school and the tactics that can get you all the way to graduation. There is even information on class preparation, job interviewing, and the actual practice of law.

However you make use of this book, be sure to pace yourself during the admissions process. In the final strategy, there is the "Get-into-Law-School Calendar." It will tell you what to do each month in order to put your applications into winning form. That calendar, along with the many other strategies, will help you make the most of *Your Ticket to Law School.*

Strategy #1

Ten Myths (and Ten Facts) About Law School Admissions

Half of what you've heard about law school may have consisted of rumor and classmate gossip. While getting into law school is no simple process, there's no need to complicate it further by listening to all the horror stories that your well-meaning classmates and relatives have to tell. There are many myths about the law school admissions process that are passed down year after year, which exist mainly to throw you off course or simply to scare you into a less challenging career. This chapter will let you in on the ten most popular myths, as well as the ten facts that are buried beneath them. Once you understand how the process really works, you'll tackle your applications with a lot more enthusiasm and a lot less anxiety.

MYTH #1: *The best method for choosing the right law school is reading the catalogs and brochures that the law admissions offices provide each year.*

FACT: While a law school's catalogs and brochures are a good source to investigate when you want to research course offerings or review the impressive list of professors, it's hardly the place where you will find a realistic appraisal of a school and its students. These catalogs are put together for one purpose: *to sell you on the school.*

Filled with pictures of ivy-covered gothic buildings, laughing students, and cheerful professors, these glossy manuals are a PR agent's dream. Many schools pay big money to have an advertising agency or in-house public relations staff design their annual catalogs and brochures. They are certainly going to quote their most illustrious alumni. They are going to put forward their own "modest" self-praise. Your job is to read through everything and pull out the hard facts that concern you, such as course offerings, campus facilities, size of library, and extracurricular activities.

Beyond the basic information found in a catalog, there are many other sources that the student should rely on when choosing a law school. One should consult the college pre-law adviser, some alumni of that particular law school, and perhaps most importantly, a few students who currently attend the law school. *The Official Pre-Law Handbook* also provides useful profiles of ABA-approved law schools. As you will discover, there are many views that the admissions catalog simply does not provide. (For more information, see Strategy #6.)

MYTH #2: *If you don't think you can get into a "top ten" law school, then maybe it isn't worth applying at all. With the current glut of lawyers, you can only get a decent job if you attend a top school.*

FACT: Close friends and relatives constantly offer advice to the college student who declares that he or she wants to attend law school. The first words the student hears are: "That's wonderful, but there's already a glut of lawyers." Don't allow yourself to be discouraged by comments like this or by suggestions that you'll never get a job unless you go to Harvard or some other top law school. It's unrealistic to think that every law firm, private corporation, foundation, department store, school system, and service organization hires its lawyers from the same ten schools.

What makes people hand out such discouraging information is not their desire to create added pressure and anxiety. It is usually their honest ignorance of the facts. Because they've read sensational headlines about three or four sensational Wall Street law firms who pay sensational salaries to the sensational students who graduate from the top ten or eleven schools, these informers suggest that all the good jobs are taken. Don't be discouraged by these remarks. Your chances of getting a good job are not only determined by which law school you attend, but also by your *grades* at that law school.

MYTH #3: *How well you score on the Law School Admissions Test (LSAT) will give you an idea of how well you will perform during law school and during your legal career.*

FACT: No matter how many important studies your roommate or pre-law adviser cites, don't believe that the Law School Admissions Test (LSAT) can predict your performance in either law school or in your legal career. This is a myth that can not only psych you out after the exam, but can scare you to death before you begin studying.

If you haven't already been told, law school is mostly reading and memorization. Your early legal career will be spent in long, back-breaking hours of late night research. How on earth can a three-hour exam predict your ability (or willingness) to do all of that? Yes, the exam tests your reading comprehension and your logical reasoning, but it cannot take into account how effective you are when it comes to spending one hundred hours preparing a legal brief. The LSAT is simply a way for the law schools to compare students from College X to those students from College Y. (For more information, see Strategy #5.)

MYTH #4: *Contacts and recommendations have almost no effect on your chances of being accepted.*

FACT: Since "contacts" has long been a dirty word in the world of academia, we'll first deal with the other half of our fourth myth: letters of recommendation. The importance of these letters cannot be stressed enough to students. If you don't already know, you should realize that there are no admissions interviews for law school. Unlike college admission officers, the law-school admissions people cannot learn about your personal qualities during a thirty-minute interview—they have to rely on what others say in a one- or two-page letter.

Letters of recommendation are treated very seriously by the law schools and students should take them seriously when they ask professors to write them.

Now, back to that word *contacts*. By now, you may have

realized that contacts can make the difference when one is in close competition for a position. Just as contacts helped that freshman-year roommate of yours who miraculously got into a college looking for SAT scores 200 points higher than his, so they can often serve you in the law school admissions process. (For more information, see Strategy #8.)

MYTH #5: *Most law schools will overlook low grades and bad LSAT scores if you had a lot of time-consuming extracurricular activities in college.*

FACT: Fat chance! You'll be hard-pressed to find a law school that will ignore low grades and low LSAT scores simply because you were sophomore-class president or feature editor of the arts journal. Yes, a good activity can make up for some of your low grades, but the only way to get the admissions officer to overlook your transcript totally is by winning a Rhodes Scholarship—and *that* you can only do with top grades!

College activities are very important, and there's a way to use them to your advantage when you've got a mediocre transcript. (For more information, see Strategy #3.)

MYTH #6: *The LSAT measures natural intelligence. Studying for it will not help you improve your score.*

FACT: Don't let anyone tell you that this three-hour exam measures your natural intelligence. It also does not measure your potential as a lawyer. This is an exam that you can both practice and study for, so don't let friends, parents, and envious classmates scare you with the suggestion that this is some sort of IQ test.

There are numerous review books to study from, and there are also special LSAT review courses that you can take for a reasonable fee. All students can improve their scores on the LSAT either by studying or by better familiarizing themselves with the rules and potential shortcuts. (For more information, see Strategy #5.)

MYTH #7: *Sending an application in early will have no effect on your chances for acceptance.*

FACT: Although each law school works differently, you can be certain that most law schools will begin looking at applications as soon as they arrive at the office. Just because the deadline date is February 1 doesn't mean that the admissions officer is going to wait until February 2 before he or she looks at applications.

Most students realize that one way of getting rejected, no matter how good their grades are, is to send in a late application. But many students don't realize that an early application might be given closer consideration because there are fewer applications to measure it against. Since the bulk of applications are sent in one or two weeks before the deadline, it may help to send yours in at least a month before the final date. This way, an admissions officer may give more time to your application than to one sent in during the final rush. It doesn't always work, but in many cases it does. (For more information, see Strategy #7.)

MYTH #8: *Sometimes it's to your advantage to bend the truth on your application. Since there are thousands of applicants, admissions officers can't possibly check up on everything you write in your application.*

FACT: This is one of the most dangerous myths. The worst thing that you can do on your application is to lie. You should avoid stretching the truth or making up stories and activities primarily because it's immoral. The second reason to avoid stretching the facts in your application is that the admissions office has ways of finding out the truth and then rejecting you, or making it difficult for you to get into any other law school.

Since honesty is one of the most important qualities of a good lawyer, law schools frown upon students who misrepresent their activities, awards, or former jobs in the application or essay. Although there is always a temptation to make up an answer when you see blank spaces on an application, you'd better remember that these admissions people weren't born yesterday. Not only will they check things out with the deans at your school if they have doubts, but they have had enough experience with various colleges to know that you were lying when you wrote that you were captain of the swim team at Walden College—when Walden doesn't even have a swim team.

There are ways of making your application *and* your activities look impressive without having to bend the truth. (For more information, see Strategy #3.)

MYTH #9: *Since so many federal scholarship and grant programs are short of money, telling a law school that you will need financial aid is almost a sure way to get yourself rejected.*

FACT: Although this is a popular belief, students should be glad to know that almost every law school has need-blind admission. This means that no matter how much financial aid you will need, this will not affect your chances of being admitted. Many students refuse to apply for financial aid because they fear that a law school will overlook their good records and reject them because they can't afford to pay the full freight.

Even if this myth were true, it would be foolish not to apply for financial aid. Let's say you did get in. How are you going to pay for the tuition if you've already led the school to believe that you don't need help? Don't try to outsmart the admissions people. Be honest with them if you have doubts—just call and ask if financial need has anything to do with admissions. (For more information, see Strategy #13.)

MYTH #10: *If you want to improve your chances for admission, don't major in math or science. Law schools prefer the student who majors in government or history.*

FACT: Our final myth is one that affects many students for two reasons. The first reason a student might feel it is better to select a major that is somewhat related to the law is that at one time (in the distant past), this was a requirement of some law schools. The other reason a student might be inclined to avoid such "unrelated" majors as math or science is just that it seems logical that these areas would be of no benefit to the future lawyer.

Currently, law schools have no required majors or courses for prospective students. Law schools look upon physics majors just as favorably as they do government majors. While medical schools might require a certain college curriculum for their applicants, pre-law students have a great deal of freedom. You will see that many law schools may even go out of their way to find students who have varied backgrounds in science, foreign languages, math, or even music. (For more information, see Strategy #2.)

Strategy #2

Taking the Right College Curriculum

In this second strategy, we have a piece of good news: law schools do not require any special college pre-law courses or major areas of study. You have complete freedom when selecting your college studies, as far as the law school's admissions office is concerned.

But while there is absolutely nothing that you *have* to know about the law or the legal system, there are certain college courses or major areas of study that may help prepare you or put you ahead of the game. Whether your school claims to offer a pre-law curriculum (if there is such a thing) or not, this chapter will give you useful suggestions on how to line up a group of courses that can give you skills to make law school less painful.

The Best Majors

Don't believe anyone who tells you that law school is going to be easy. Not only does it require that you devote long hours to the memorization of certain facts, but it requires that you use certain skills that few of us were born with and which most of us must pick up somewhere along the way.

Ten or fifteen years ago, the typical pre-law student would major in a department like history, politics, or criminal justice. This was done because there seemed to be a logical connection between law school and those three areas of study. Today, law schools readily accept students who majored in such subjects as chemistry, music, religion, and English. You must realize that *there are no specific majors which are certain to improve your chances of admission*—they can only (at most) aid you in your future legal studies. To emphasize this point, let's look at what happened to Liza.

Liza was a very ambitious college student who'd wanted to be a lawyer ever since she'd seen her first episode of *Perry Mason.* During her first two semesters, she took a variety of courses including psychology, government, English literature, and sociology. Although she had received her worst grades in the two government courses, when it came time to choose a major, she went ahead and selected government. Now, some of you might cheer Liza on for being so courageous as to pursue a major in an area she found so difficult. But here is why Liza was at fault:

Liza did not choose government as a major because she liked it—actually she hated it. She found her psychology, English, and sociology courses much more interesting, but being the ambitious, legal-minded student that she was, Liza felt that law schools would be more impressed if she chose a major that seemed lawyerlike. What was so foolish about her choice was that she selected a major for which she had no real feeling—her grades were much higher in every other department.

Even *if* a law school approves your choice of a "lawyerlike" major, it would be much happier to see a transcript with a major course load that earned high grades. Since Liza majored in an area which she disliked and scored poorly in, she ended up with a transcript full of low grades—definitely a strike against her. Select a major that you enjoy and in which you will perform well. If you feel compelled to, you can always decide to take one or two of those extra courses that you believe will enhance your law school applications.

As mentioned earlier, there are no particular majors that will improve your chances for law school admission. But there are a few majors that may better prepare you for legal study. Some of these are: mathematics, philosophy, political science, English, and journalism.

The reason math and philosophy can be beneficial is that both train you to think logically—a talent which is very useful in law school, as well as in a legal career. Law school requires students to focus on specific problems and to take them apart—almost as one would do with a math equation or a philosophic argument.

As for political science, one has the opportunity to learn about political systems. Though this does not form the basis of a law school curriculum, it is an important component in understanding why certain laws are developed, and how different governments utilize them.

Perhaps the most useful major areas of study for pre-law students are English or journalism. This is because law schools are finding that fewer and fewer students in recent years are able to write well. While law schools are certainly not searching for the next Hemingway or Fitzgerald, they want students who can express themselves clearly and succinctly, and analyze issues on paper. Many journalism students develop the skill of focusing their writing without making numerous drafts. You will understand how valuable this talent can be once you compete for law review or are faced with having to draft your first brief.

Liberal Arts Vs. Science/Engineering

If you are worried that an engineering degree is not looked upon as favorably as a liberal arts degree, relax. Although relatively few engineers choose to become lawyers, law schools encourage students from these disciplines just as much as they encourage students who've studied liberal arts.

Engineers may decide to attend law school because they plan to enter a certain field of law that allows them to use their engineering knowledge and skills. Not only are there mechanical, chemical, and electrical engineering companies in need of their own in-house attorneys, but there are many law firms that specialize in or represent companies who would benefit from having a lawyer with an engineering background.

Courses That Teach Good Legal Skills

Just as there are certain major areas of study that can provide you with good legal skills, there are specific college courses that can better prepare you for law school. They include Constitutional Interpretation, one of the few truly law-school-like courses that is offered at some universities. Such a course usually teaches the student to closely analyze the U.S. Constitution and a few very significant judicial decisions. Since many law schools offer a wide variety of courses under the heading of "Constitutional Law," an early background in this area can help.

Another college course that will aid you is Introductory Logic. Not only is logic an important skill for law school, but it is also essential for the LSAT. There are at least two sections on this exam that test your logical reasoning abilities. Most colleges offer at least one or two logic courses in their philosophy departments.

Another course which may be very beneficial to you as a future law student is one which not only requires you to write papers, but that makes great demands on your reading skills. In law school you will have to be prepared to write frequently, and you will have daily reading assignments. By "daily," law schools really mean *every single day*. Most upper-level English courses can prepare you for the constant reading assignments you will be faced with during three years of law school.

Graded Vs. Pass/Fail Courses

When selecting your college courses each semester, keep in mind that the law schools will be noting your grades before anything else on your transcript. Even if your college allows you to take as many pass/fail courses as you like, law schools are not going to look kindly on a transcript full of P grades. The law school has to rank its candidates, and it needs to know if your passing grade was an A-plus or a C-minus. At the same time, however, it may be to your advantage to opt for the P if you think you're on your way to getting a C-minus.

One good rule is to utilize the pass/fail option as infrequently as possible. Even the American Bar Association says that a student with a large number of pass/fail grades is making the selection process more tedious for the law-school admissions people. If your college requires that you take thirty-two courses during the four years, it may be wise to limit yourself to no more than four pass/fail courses—and for the very best law schools, you may want to limit yourself to just two or three.

Sometimes students find themselves panicking under the stress of a very important course, and quickly change the grading option to pass/fail, only to find out later that they received an A on the final exam. If this happens to you, and you really would like to let the law school know what your letter grade *would* have been, you might ask your professor to send a note explaining your average. Some admissions people will take this into consideration when they are judging your file.

Summer Courses

Some colleges offer a six- or seven-week pre-law summer program for college students (usually between their junior and senior years) both to enhance student applications and to better prepare students for what they will face in law school. One of the most prominent of these programs is offered at Cornell University in Ithaca, New York.

While these programs may have no effect on your chances for admission, they will frequently teach you how to prepare for the LSAT and introduce you to various areas of the legal profession by inviting practicing attorneys and other speakers to the campus. Ask your pre-law adviser or career placement officer for applications to these programs if you are interested.

Techniques to Cultivate

In addition to selecting courses that provide good legal skills, there are many special techniques that you can learn outside the college classroom. These techniques may offer practical help as you face a rigorous course load in law school. Some of these techniques include: note-taking, outlining, speed-reading, memorization, and operating word processors.

At first you may feel that everything your law professor says is important. Some students walk out of a one-hour lecture with twenty pages of notes. This might seem impressive, but it's foolhardy. There is a secret to note-taking—and it doesn't include writing down every word the professor speaks. There are books that explain how to identify what's important in a lecture. Learning this skill will save you both time and the pain of writer's cramp. Another important talent to develop is knowing how to make outlines. The most useful method of exam study requires the ability to compose clear, concise outlines from lecture notes and reading material.

Speed-reading and memorization are skills taught in adult education programs and by commercial groups. Since there is generally at least four hours of reading required each day in law school, learning to read quickly and to remember what you've read will help you study more efficiently. Finally, a working knowledge of word processors may help you during your three years of law school. Preparing legal briefs is a tedious chore that all students must perform, and these machines can save a lot of time.

Strategy #3

Activities That Will Strengthen Your Application

You have probably heard that grades and test scores aren't the only components in the law school's selection process. Students should realize that law schools are extremely interested in the extracurricular activities of their applicants. Because admissions people are looking at a student's well-roundedness, they want to learn about talents that are displayed outside the classroom.

You should by no means rush out and join a dozen college or off-campus activities simply because you want to fill in all the spaces on your law school application. But realize that many students with high grades and high scores have been rejected because they had no activities or outside interests to balance their records. Although one can't get into a good law school on the strength of an activity alone, there's almost no way to assemble a strong application without it.

No matter which activity or activities you participate in in college, keep in mind that more is not always better. Being able to list your membership in eight or nine clubs is not as impressive as being able to list an important position with one. The best rule is to take part in those activities that interest you. Whether it's the debate squad, the yearbook staff, student government, or the basketball team, you should choose it because you enjoy it. Since you may end up staying with the activity from freshman year until you graduate, it's not wise participating in something you dislike.

When Julia decided in her sophomore year that she wanted to pursue a career in international law, she signed up for the French Club. Although she disliked the language and had already suffered through two years of French, she felt that law schools would be impressed with her membership in a foreign-language club—especially when she explained that her interests were in international law. Maybe some of the law schools would have been impressed. But was it worth the anxiety that Julia had to suffer every time she had to face another French Club meeting or event? I doubt it.

If you join a club or activity that you dislike, you will probably never perform well or earn a high position in the group. If you don't reach a leadership position in any of your activities, the law schools will assume that you spent very little time on them. If the law schools believe that you spent little time on your activities, your application will be just as unimpressive as that of the student who never joined any clubs or activities. The point of this should be clear to you: try to join an activity where you can eventually gain a leadership position.

You should try to focus on just two or three activities in the beginning, then later decide on the one to which you would like to devote the most time. If you choose any more than this, you'll spread yourself too thin and find yourself not giving enough time to the most important thing—your class work.

Student Government

This is a favorite choice of the pre-law student. You might be surprised to know just how many law-school applicants have been involved in student government in some way. This is not to say that becoming class president is the sure way to get into law school. But one reason it's so popular a choice of pre-law students is it's political, and many college politicos want to be lawyers.

When Peter entered college, he joined several freshman-class committees of the student government. Certain that he would eventually want to be president of either his class or the entire student body, he figured he would start small and try to meet as many people as possible. After becoming the chairperson of two class committees, Peter ran for one of the four delegate positions in his sophomore year. As sophomore class delegate, he had more power, additional responsibility, and greater name recognition on the campus. At the end of sophomore year, several students who saw how involved and dedicated Peter was started a campaign to elect him president of the junior class.

Near the end of his term as junior-class president, Peter's ambitions grew and he campaigned to become vice-president of the student body. Because he had so many loyal supporters and because most other students had read about his activities in the school newspaper, Peter had no problem winning the election. When it was time for Peter to complete his law school applications, he emphasized his political experience. The law schools were very impressed with Peter's steady climb and his consistent interest in campus government.

What all students should realize, though, is that the fact that Peter held all those positions, alone, is not going to win over the admissions people. What is most important is the way in which he discusses his activities in his application (what he learned from the activity, what he accomplished, how all this fits in with law school and his future). If he raises all of these points, then he's really shown why the activity is important.

School Newspaper and Publications

Another popular activity for many pre-law students is working on the campus newspaper. This activity can be extremely beneficial to the law-school applicant. Not only can you learn important journalistic writing skills (a useful talent for law school) on the paper, but you will also have samples of your activity to send with your application. Unlike many students, a newspaper editor can substantiate the quality of his activity with actual printed articles. A member of student government can only say that he or she did a good job on the application. An editor or reporter can prove it with samples.

When Crystal joined her campus weekly, she enthusiastically took on the most challenging writing assignments. As she rose through the ranks on the staff, her controversial stories attracted great attention and even won her some awards. Any law school would have been impressed with Crystal's eventual position as editor-in-chief, but what made her especially desirable was her talent for writing and her decision to take on important issues. Ultimately, every law student is expected to take on important issues in his or her career. Crystal simply gave herself a good head start.

Model United Nations/Debate Team

Both of these groups focus on current issues. While a college Model U.N. organization will deal with international issues, a debate team may focus on just about any topic. The benefits of belonging to either of these organizations starts with the fact that members are taught to research issues in great depth. No matter what the topic is, members are expected to research and present their arguments professionally. In many ways, this format might be compared to moot court—an important law school activity used to teach students how to argue a case.

The law schools know that only the most serious students take part in this activity. Popularity is generally not a motivation for joining—an honest interest in current topics is what keeps these students active.

Once you've begun to fill out your applications, you might want to highlight your performance on the debate team by listing your meets and sending photocopies of your awards or citations. If you filled a staff position while with the Model U.N., send the law schools a copy of the program from one of your recent conferences.

Pre-Law Society

Although this statement may offend some, this is an activity that almost shouts, "Hey, look at me—I want to be a lawyer!" Most college campuses have a pre-law society which invites important lecturers to campus to speak about legal issues or topics that would be of special concern to pre-law students. Although there are generally four or five extremely busy officers who direct each of these groups, becoming a member won't take up much of your time. If your campus doesn't have a pre-law society, start one. In addition to learning about organizing your own activity, you'll be able to tell the law schools that you were the founder.

Athletic Activities

Although there is no real connection between sports and law school, there are many athletes who apply for admission. One word to student athletes, though: if your grades and scores are low, belonging to a sports team is one of the activities that will mean the least to the admissions people (no matter how many goals or points you racked up for the season). Putting it simply, athletic activities cannot make up for low grades as being news editor for the campus daily might. Aside from that, however, there are many benefits to be obtained from participating in a sport. Not only do you become well rounded, but you get the chance to work with a team while also having fun.

What an athlete should emphasize in his application are the things that he has learned from group competition, as well as the things that he has learned from solo competition in the classroom. A member of any sports team probably has a better idea of what it means to work with others than most campus politicos do. Highlight this point in the essay.

Social Causes

Whether you're organizing a task force on women's rights or a fund-raising drive to send food to an impoverished area, working for a social cause while you're on campus can be very meaningful, both to you and to any law school you tell about it. Those students who dedicate themselves to helping others or educating fellow students about important issues are perhaps the most valuable in the eyes of most law schools. These students are not only serious, but they are clearly concerned individuals who don't need the glamor of politics or the crowds at athletic events to find satisfaction.

No matter what motives you have for joining a social cause, you provide a balance against some of the more self-interested students who frequently apply to law school.

Other Activities

Dramatics, fraternities/sororities, entrepreneurial groups, and music organizations are some of the many other activities that are available to college students. None of these were highlighted because they are not directly related to the interests of most pre-law students. This is not to say that you should not participate in them. No matter which college activities interest you, there's a way to discuss them in your application and to explain how you've benefited from them. What will truly aid your application is not the name of the activity, the real value is in what you have contributed and learned from the time you've invested.

Strategy #4

Work Experience: How It Applies

In addition to your extracurricular activities, law schools are also particularly interested in your on-campus and off-campus employment record. You may ask why work experience would be considered important. The answer is because it makes you stand out from other student applicants. For that reason, this strategy will cover the types of summer and term-time jobs that can be valuable both because they support your application and because they can teach you useful skills for law school.

Summer Jobs

Most college students choose to work during the summer, for a variety of reasons. Many work to earn money to pay for tuition and school expenses. Some use the experience to strengthen their resumes, and still others take summer jobs in order to make career decisions or learn about a certain field. Whatever your reasons for seeking summer employment, you should remember that the law schools will always ask you how you spent your summers. You are certainly entitled to spend some time lying on the beach and relaxing, but carefully selected summer employment can play an important role in making your law-school application stronger in the eyes of the admissions office.

The following are examples of two extremes to avoid when making your own summer plans.

By the time Alex began his senior year in high school, he'd decided that his future lay in a legal career. While this was an early point at which to reach such a major decision, Alex was the kind of student who likes to have his future planned early and rarely deviates from his plans unless required to by unforeseen circumstances. Alex had made his decision, and he was determined to make all the right choices for the next four years so that he could get into a top law school after college.

The first summer job Alex arranged was one in his county's legal department. Since he had only just graduated from high school, he believed (and rightly so) that it would be difficult to find a summer job in a good law firm, especially one with a national reputation or famous clients. While the duties he performed were not particularly interesting, Alex had an impressive resume even before he entered college.

The following summer Alex worked as an intern in a Congressman's office. Though the position was menial, and his duties just a cut above those of a messenger, Alex knew he should stick out the summer because a political internship looks good on a law-school application.

Alex thought about using his savings to take a trip to Europe during the summer after his sophomore year, but he worried that such a vacation wouldn't add sufficiently to his credentials. Deciding that he could travel some other time, he instead took a job at a well-known New York law firm. Not only would he be getting a closer look at the profession, but he'd probably pick up some legal skills and maybe even a prestigious name for his list of references.

Alex reached the summer of his junior year thinking once more about riding bikes through Europe with a couple of friends. But, succumbing to pressure from his parents and his insecurities about getting into a top-ten law school, he chose to spend the summer in a job that would make his resume stand out in a sea of superior applications. He looked over his list of summer jobs and saw "County Legal Office," "Congressional Intern," and "Intern for Wall Street Attorney." It was an impressive list, but Alex decided something was missing. He felt it was something charitable, humanitarian—so he applied for, and got, a job working for the Legal Aid Society.

Alex got into the law school of his choice. The admissions office was impressed by the way he'd spent his summers, and Alex felt secure that he had done all the right things to reach his goal. He never did take that trip to Europe, though, and, to this day, Alex is still locked into his need to choose prestige over pleasure.

Susan was an average student majoring in art history in college, and, while she had no clear career choice in mind, she had always figured on applying to law school someday, just as her older sister had. Susan's pre-law adviser had suggested she try to improve her chances for admission by carefully selecting her summer jobs to show her interest in the legal profession. But Susan hated the idea of being confined to an office all day, and figured that she'd be able to get in with good grades, decent LSAT scores, and recommendations from teachers who liked her.

So what did Susan do during her college summers? The summer before freshman year she scooped ice cream in a snack bar by the local beach. The following year she got a job as a mother's helper with a family going to Nantucket. The summer after her sophomore year she took a position as lifeguard at the neighborhood swimming pool. When the summer after junior year beckoned, Susan recalled her adviser's advice about using summer jobs to strengthen her law school applications, but she had her heart set on a trip to Italy, which she saw as one last fling before starting the grind of graduate school.

What Susan hadn't counted on, however, was that her grade point average was lower than she expected, her LSAT score was only fair, and her recommendations from professors were modest ones. She was lucky to get into her last-choice law school, considering the odds against her, but she'd thoroughly enjoyed all the fun summers she'd had during college. Would more careful choice of summer jobs have made a real difference on her applications? *Possibly.* Summer employment is just part of the whole picture you offer the admissions officers. Try to find a balance between Alex and Susan's stories that will give you the best shot possible at getting into the law school of your choice.

Part-Time Jobs

Like many college students, you may find yourself in need of an on-campus job during the school year. Most students find that ten to fifteen hours a week is the most they can take on, especially with a full course load. There are usually many opportunities for term-time jobs, so you may as well try to find a position that will provide you with more than a weekly paycheck. Instead of taking a job in the dining hall, you may be able to find one as research assistant to a professor in your department, or a staff position in the library. Jobs that train you to use office equipment such as word processors or computers can also add to the resume you're building.

The Job-Experience-to-Application Connection

After you've managed to build a list of job experiences, the most important thing to do is make it pay off on your law school applications. Try to be realistic about using facts to best advantage on the applications. When summarizing your work experience, always be honest, but make your work sound as substantial as possible.

There's a way to "dress up" every job without having to stretch the truth. If the long hours you've put in are the most impressive thing about a particular job, stress them. If you're working for a well-known figure in any line of work, stress that. Always make the most of what you've done, and relate it to the development of stronger personal skills and habits.

If you've had to speak before groups as part of a job, even if it's just to introduce speakers or give instructions to other volunteers, mention that. There is much to learn on any job that may not be in the job description, and law-school admissions officers are sincerely interested in the personal growth a candidate has experienced in the working world.

There are many other summer or part-time positions that were not mentioned in this chapter. Here are some of the groups and institutions that offer jobs for the pre-law student that can add both depth and variety to any resume.

- *political campaigns:* advance person, public relations
- *law offices:* clerical position (filing, typing)
- *law library:* categorizing or anything else that teaches you about legal research

- *city, county, state, federal government:* intern for any of the many agencies
- *environmental groups:* researcher, organizer to distribute information
- *corporate businesses:* office intern, research intern, work that teaches business operations
- *legal-aid groups:* community liaison
- *nonprofit organizations:* volunteer, paid intern
- *civic groups:* clerical position, organizer of drives, workshops
- *publishing companies:* editorial assistant or other jobs that improve writing and reading skills
- *educational institution:* student teacher, research assistant to professor or dean

Strategy #5

The LSAT and How to Study for It

The Law School Admission Test (LSAT) is probably the greatest cause of fear for students who are beginning the application process. They have heard all sorts of rumors on what the test measures, how one must prepare, how it is scored, as well as how many lives it will ruin each year. This chapter will clear up these rumors and provide tips to help you prepare for the test.

It has been often claimed that the LSAT can predict your performance in law school. Don't believe it. It is simply one measure of your ability to think and solve problems in a careful and logical way. Just like the SAT that you took in high school, this test can be prepared for with special reviewing. Although you may already have some of the talents that it takes to perform well with the questions, it is by no means an exam which measures natural intelligence.

Generally administered four times each year (March, June, October, and December), this seven-part exam consists of six 35-minute multiple-choice sections and one half-hour essay. The four-hour exam is scored on a scale of 10 to 50, and presents four different types of multiple choice questions. With the revision of the exam in 1982, the LSAT no longer features quantitative math.

Types of Multiple-Choice Problems and How to Answer Them

The different categories of multiple-choice questions have no formal titles, but many students label them as Facts and Issues,

Reading Comprehension, Logic Games, and Logical Reasoning. The other two sections of the six are experimental—a repeated version of any of the four question types—and will not be counted against you. Since you aren't told which ones are experimental, you simply must work at your greatest potential throughout the entire exam.

Facts and Issues

These are probably the simplest questions on the exam, as well as the quickest to solve. Because of the constant time pressure, it will be to your advantage to get this section near the end of the LSAT, when you're exhausted.

Facts and Issues presents problems that appear similar to those of a lawyer. You are given some facts, a dispute, two rules, and possible questions that might apply to the problem. After reading all of the information, you are to analyze the questions like a lawyer, and classify each *question* under one of four headings: A) Relevant, but answer requires a choice between the rules; B) Relevant, but answer requires more facts; C) Relevant, and readily answerable; D) Irrelevant question.

Although all of this may seem confusing now, it won't be once you begin practicing with actual problems. Working with this section is almost like pretending to be a judge. You don't answer the questions that someone is asking about a case. You simply decide if the questions are relevant or not. One of the secrets to doing well on this section is practicing the questions and memorizing the directions. The directions will always tell you to answer either *A*, *B*, *C*, or *D*—these answer choices will always be the same for each question. Once you memorize the four choices, as well as the distinctions between each choice, you can save a considerable amount of time.

It's important that you work through the Facts and Issues section methodically. One effective way to proceed with the questions in this section is as follows:

1. Read the rules *first*.
2. Determine the distinction between the two rules given.
3. Read the facts carefully.
4. Proceed to the question.
5. Ask yourself, is the question *relevant* to the facts? If not, your answer is automatically *D*. If the question is relevant, then continue.

6. Is the question readily answerable based upon the facts and rules provided? If so, the answer is *C*.
7. Does answering the question require a choice between the rules? If so, the answer is *A*.
8. Does answering the question require additional facts or rules? If so, the answer is *B*.

This is obviously only one way in which to proceed with the Facts and Issues section. However, by establishing this sort of methodical procedure, you will be able to solve each problem quickly and efficiently. And finally, there are a few general things you should keep in mind:

- Remember that the rules and facts given, as well as the questions asked, do not presuppose *any* legal knowledge whatsoever.
- Each question must be solved independently of all the other questions.
- Be particularly aware of words that subtly shift the meaning of the question, such as *only*, *some*, *except*, *provided that*, *may be*, *unless*, *as many as*, and so on.

Reading Comprehension

You probably remember a similar section on the SAT from when you were in high school. Well, it hasn't really changed except that the paragraphs have gotten longer and more tedious. Here you will be given a passage of approximately three paragraphs, which is followed by several questions that test your comprehension from memory, but you also are required to draw certain conclusions from the material that you have read.

At this point it may seem simple, but be warned that it isn't. Not only are the passages long, but some are extremely technical and boring. They will not be charming stories of fiction. They will be paragraphs excerpted from various publications such as science journals, history books, and collections of criticism. In other words, they are written so that you have to *force* yourself to concentrate. And no matter how intelligent you are, the only way to answer the questions that follow is to read the paragraph *actively*, memorizing and underlining important details as you go. You should never rely on previous knowledge. The questions are tricky and they will give you choices that are designed to confuse you.

Here are a few things to keep in mind when working on the Reading Comprehension section:

- *Before* reading the passage, quickly skim the question stems, circling any key phrases.
- Then read the passage carefully with the questions in mind. Read actively, noting particularly the first sentence of each paragraph, and marking key words, phrases, and dates.
- Don't overmark. It will distract you. Only highlight the key idea(s) in each paragraph.
- If statistics are used, it's often to highlight only the highest and lowest figures given.
- Answer the questions as quickly and as accurately as possible, without referring back to the passage unless absolutely necessary.
- When considering the answer choices for each question, be sure to eliminate immediately any unreasonable or obviously incorrect answer choice.

One way to prepare yourself for these problems is to start reading the most tedious articles or magazines that you can find at home or in the library. There is rarely enough time on the test to read the passage more than once, so you should become accustomed to reading things that you don't particularly enjoy. It's a lot like law school!

Logic Games

Games is the wrong word here. There have never been harder questions on an exam. If you find this section to be as enjoyable as a game, then you should make a terrific lawyer. These questions are designed to test your ability to use logic to determine the relationships between objects. The people who do well on this section are usually those who have mathematical minds. And although quantitative math was removed from the LSAT, this is the *qualitative* math that stayed in.

With these problems you will be given a set of relationships and conditions, and asked several questions which require you to work out the exact relationship of one object to another. You've probably seen these problems before. Here's an example:

— Five people are standing in a line.
— Each person is wearing shoes and socks.
— Their shoes are either green loafers, white boots, or red high heels.
— Their socks are red, white, or blue.
— Any one person cannot be wearing the same color shoes and socks.
— Two adjacent people cannot be wearing the same shoes.
— Two adjacent people cannot be wearing the same color socks.
— No more than two pairs of any color shoes or socks may be worn at the same time.

Question: If the 1st and 3rd persons are wearing white boots, and the 2nd and 4th persons have on blue socks, which of the following *must* be true?

(A) the 4th person is wearing green loafers
(B) the 1st person is wearing blue socks
(C) the 5th person is wearing white socks
(D) there is one pair of red high heels
(E) the 3rd person is wearing white socks

The correct answer is *C*.

Easy, isn't it? Most people draw a blank when they first read these problems. The secret to answering this kind of question often lies in drawing up simple charts or diagrams that help clarify the physical relationships between the given objects. For the problem above, your diagram might look something like this:

Shoes: green loafers (gl); white boots (wb); red high heels (rh)
Socks: red socks (rs); white socks (ws); blue socks (bs)
Conditions: no same colors together, no same colors adjacent, two pairs each max.

People:	(1)	(2)	(3)	(4)	(5)
Shoes:	wb	rh/gl	wb	rh/gl	rh/gl
Socks:	rs	bs	rs	bs	ws

By diagramming the problem in this fashion, you can quickly establish the various possible relationships between the given objects. The review books and/or the test preparation courses explain this method in detail.

Logical Reasoning

By now, you've probably decided that law school is not for you. Don't be scared away so easily. This next section of the exam is relatively straightforward. As the heading suggests, the questions measure your ability to reason. There is great value to mastering these questions. Through them, you'll learn how to structure and analyze your arguments once you begin law school.

For instance, you might be given a very short syllogism:

> Emily is a mother. All mothers are smart. Therefore Emily is smart.

This is followed by five additional syllogisms as answer choices:

(A) All race cars are fast. Jim's go-cart is fast. Therefore Jim's go-cart might be a race car.
(B) You are a rational being. All rational beings are good at logical reasoning. Therefore you are good at logical reasoning.
(C) Because Emily is smart and all smart people are mothers, Emily must be a mother.
(D) All dogs smell. This animal doesn't smell. Therefore this animal isn't a dog.
(E) Paper beats rock, but scissors beat paper. Therefore scissors beat rock.

Your job will be to decide which of the five answer choices uses the same kind of reasoning as the sample argument. The answer is *B*.

Other types of logical reasoning questions can be a little more challenging. For example, you might be given a passage which has words missing, and be asked which one of a group of possible phrases most logically fits into the paragraph. In this example the answer is *C*.

He who gives himself entirely to his fellow men appears to them useless and selfish; but he who gives himself partially to them is pronounced ______________________.

(A) shortsighted and timid
(B) a thoughtless fool
(C) a benefactor and philanthropist
(D) a true patriot
(E) unworthy of his citizenship

Another common form of question that you will find in the Logical Reasoning section involves author identification, in which you are asked to identify the most likely author of a given passage. Or you might be given a series of five related sentences listed in random order, which you must rearrange into the most logical sequence. This kind of problem might look something like this:

I. But he could not help making Him give a shove to set the world in motion.
II. Such beliefs are inconsistent and unacceptable.
III. He would have liked to be able to bypass God.
IV. After that he had nothing to do with God.
V. I cannot forgive Descartes.

The most logical order would be:
(A) III, II, IV, I, V
(B) V, III, I, IV, II
(C) II, IV, V, III, I
(D) I, V, III, II, IV
(E) III, V, IV, I, II

The answer is *B*.

There are over a dozen different types of questions that you are likely to encounter in this section. The examples given here are provided simply to give you a general idea of what you can expect to find in the Logical Reasoning section of the LSAT. In general, you should remember to:

- Read the question first, so that you know exactly what you're looking for when reading the passage or argument that precedes the answer choices.

- Watch for irrelevant or obviously incorrect answer choices and eliminate them immediately.
- Read *actively*, and pay particular attention to subtle qualifiers, such as *must, might, none, all*, and *only*.

The Essay

You will have thirty minutes in which to write an essay. You will be given a topic at the beginning of the exam on which you must write a well-structured argument. The topic is usually a controversial issue of some sort, for instance, Should the legal drinking age be raised to twenty-one years of age? You won't need to have any prior knowledge of the topic.

The purpose of this writing sample is to take a position on a given topic and to back it up with logical arguments. You don't have to use facts at all. But you should keep a few things in mind when you write the essay. It is important that your essay be well organized and well written. Begin by drawing up a brief outline of what you want to say. But remember that you are limited by time, so don't get involved in an overly long and complicated discussion. Your best essay will have a thesis, followed by three main points justifying your position or thesis. You are not scored on the essay. The law schools are only going to read it (some don't even look at it) in order to see if you know how to write logically and grammatically.

Law School Data Assembly Service (LSDAS)

This is the service that you should register with when you sign up to take the LSAT. In addition to keeping your LSAT scores on file, the LSDAS obtains your college transcripts, summarizes them, and then releases them to the various law schools to which you've applied. When you apply to the law schools, you have to send off a series of postcards supplied by the LSDAS. There are two different postcards for each school to which you apply. One is sent out as soon as you receive it from the LSDAS. It goes to each school from which you are requesting a transcript. The second card must be included with each of your applications to law school. This will all be explained in greater detail when you've received your registration packet. For more information about registering for the LSAT/LSDAS, you should write to Law School Admission Service, Box 2000, Newtown, PA 18940.

Review Books and Test Preparation Courses

Use both if you can afford them. Many people take a seven-week or three-week crash course with one of the tutoring services. Stanley H. Kaplan Educational Center and Sexton Educational Services are two of the largest nationwide organizations that offer preparatory courses for the LSAT. Although taking courses can be expensive, they provide you with knowledgeable teachers, practice booklets, and tape recordings that will explain the answers to LSAT questions. In addition to meeting in a classroom on a daily or weekly basis, you can practice with the tapes and review material during your spare time.

As for the review books, they are a must for everyone. You will find a list of LSAT review books in the bibliography.

It's essential that you familiarize yourself with the four types of test questions. You'll be taking the test under great time constraints, so you should be, at the very least, familiar with the directions for each type of problem—they're always the same. And remember, almost everyone studies for the LSAT. Don't put yourself at an early disadvantage.

Test-Taking Strategies

Probably the best pre-exam strategy is practicing with a copy of the actual LSAT. In recent years, copies of past exams have been released, and your pre-law adviser or the test preparation services should have a copy available. Be sure to take the exam under the time limits and conditions of an actual testing situation and see how you do. This is much more realistic than using just the sample questions from a review book.

Strategies to follow on the day of the exam:

- Try to sleep seven to eight hours during the night before the exam. If you sleep any longer, you'll be lethargic.
- If your exam is in the morning, as it usually is, wake up at least two hours before it begins.
- Bring a snack with you that you can eat during your exam break. Bring high-protein foods like nuts, or fruit.
- Don't sit near nervous and fidgety people during the test. And don't talk to them during the break.
- Don't be afraid to complain if the room is too hot or too cold. It will affect your performance.
- Always ask questions if there is a problem with your test booklet or answer sheet.
- Try to sit next to a wall so that you can turn away from any distractions.
- Bring every possible comfort that will save you time (extra pencils, pencil sharpener, tissues).
- Don't try to show off by finishing first—no one cares.

If, for some reason, you feel sure that you performed poorly on the exam, you can cancel it. But you must do this immediately—you don't have the option of seeing your score and then cancelling it. While the law schools will know that you cancelled the test, it's better to take it again when you're more confident. Don't listen to people who say that it looks bad on your record. There are students who have taken the LSAT three times and then gotten into the top law schools. Do what's best for you. Good luck!

Strategy #6

Deciding Where to Apply

Choosing the right law school is just as important as choosing the right college. Every law school is different—some are large, some are very expensive, some are extremely competitive, and some offer a wider curriculum than others.

The best way to start is to make a list of the law schools that you've heard something about. When students think about law schools, they often think of Harvard or Yale, but there are many more to consider. If you're not familiar with any in particular, it might be best to look through a complete list of them (see the appendix) and then send away for catalogs from some of the schools. If your college has a counseling office on campus, it should have an open collection of catalogs for you to read.

Many students like to glance through one of the large directories, like *The Official Pre-Law Handbook* from the College Board, in order to find out each school's recommended grade point averages and LSAT scores. Although the book does not tell how to apply, it will give you an idea of the median grades and scores for the different schools.

Once you have compiled a list of approximately twenty-five schools, check them against the following factors to consider when deciding where to apply.

Your Grades and LSAT Scores

Whenever you read about the recommended grade averages and LSAT scores for particular schools, remember that these numbers are usually mean figures. In other words, you are being given a midpoint to gauge your own chances for admission. Although many law schools will list the recommended grades and scores in their separate catalogs, some are reluctant to give you any indication whatsoever. Since these grades and scores are never exact, a school that lists a B-plus average will accept a certain number of B and B-minus students, just as they will accept a certain number of A-minus and A students.

Although you should use your grades and scores as a guide to select most of the schools in your pool of applications, don't be afraid to also apply to those that are above your range. You may have some other notable strength in your application which will compensate for a low score or grade point average.

Prestige of the School

Many pre-law students consider prestige a major factor in deciding to apply to certain law schools. Although there is no formal list of "prestige" schools, these law schools would probably be among the top twenty-five or thirty in the country—including Harvard, Stanford, Yale, Chicago, Columbia, Berkeley, Georgetown, University of Pennsylvania, and a number of others.

What is the actual value of the prestige schools? In addition to having established names, these schools generally feature a broad curriculum, have outstanding professors, and have very good records for placing students in jobs with the top law firms nationwide. But remember, there are plenty of excellent and middle-range law schools that offer a fine education and can suit your needs. Don't let prestige become your sole criterion for applying to a particular school.

Location of the School

A school's location is another prime factor in your decision to apply. Here, location refers to both setting and distance from home.

If you grew up in a rural setting and attended a college or

university out in the country, you might find it difficult to attend a law school in the center of a major city. Of course, if you're going to practice certain kinds of law, it might be wise to grow accustomed to city life as soon as you can. You also may not want the distractions that a busy city offers. In addition to dealing with crowds and traffic, you may face the difficulties of traveling from library to dormitory at night through neighborhoods considered unsafe to all but the streetwise. This may seem unimportant now, but once you begin law school, you'll wish you had taken the time to consider this factor.

If you are accustomed to city life, you may find problems adjusting to a rural campus. Although class work will take up most of your time, you may miss the welcome distraction and entertainment that larger cities will offer.

When students consider distance, they usually have two concerns on their minds. They may be worried about the cost of traveling cross country to a law school or about whether it's foolish to attend a school in a state where they never plan to practice law. The first point is important, because although the school year does not offer many vacations when you can go home, travel costs and moving expenses can be quite prohibitive. Add to that your long-distance phone bills and you'll see how expensive it can be to attend schools that are a great distance from home.

As for attending a law school near where you someday hope to practice, don't be too concerned. Law firms have a wide network for interviewing and recruiting students.

Curriculum

Though you may not have realized it, every law school does not offer the same curriculum. Although first-year law students generally take the same courses (Contracts, Constitutional Interpretation, and others), second- and third-year law students must choose electives which relate to their special interests. It's a good idea to look over the course catalogs for the schools that interest you. If you're interested in becoming an entertainment lawyer, it's foolish to apply to schools that don't offer courses appropriate for that field. Of course, you may not have any idea of what area you will select yet, but it is always better to attend a law school that offers a wide variety of second- and third-year law courses.

Quality of Facilities

Another consideration should be the quality of the law school's facilities. This applies to the law library as well as to dormitory housing and the career placement office. The best way to investigate these three areas is either by writing to the library, the housing office, and the career placement office and asking for literature, or, even better, by visiting the campus and seeing the facilities first-hand.

No matter how great a school's reputation is, the facilities that it offers are a most important consideration to you. If the library has a limited number of volumes, the quality of your research will be limited. If dormitory space is at a minimum, you may be forced to live off campus and commute from great distances. And some career placement offices may not offer the types of counseling services that you may need in order to be assured of finding the best summer jobs or selecting the right field of law for you. All of these things are important.

The Law Library

The library is a vitally important facility no matter where you attend law school. It's essential to look into the quality of its resources. Many students judge the quality of a library by noting the number of volumes it has. While it may be unfair to say that a good school has lots of books and a bad school has only a few books, one can safely say that your potential for research will be greater if you have a greater number of volumes with which to work.

In terms of one's ability to perform the highest quality of research, one might say that the very best law school libraries have at least 375 thousand volumes. This number can only be found in a handful of the most prestigious law schools. The next tier of law schools should have at least 225 thousand volumes. A school which has fair to good resources should probably have at least 100 thousand volumes in its library. Most law school graduates would agree that a law library with fewer than 50 thousand volumes is simply underdeveloped and not sufficient to provide students with the books and resources that they need.

Tuition and Other Costs

There is another major factor to consider as you apply to particular law schools. Since the cost of a legal education can vary greatly from one school to another, the amount of money that you and your parents are willing to spend will also help determine which law schools you can attend. While there are state law schools that charge only a couple thousand dollars each year, there are some prestigious and private law schools which demand well over $15,000.

Before eliminating the more expensive schools from consideration, figure out all of your financial resources. There are grant and loan programs that can help you. In strategy thirteen of this book, there is information on how to find grants, loans, and private scholarships that are awarded both to students who can show need and to those who cannot. Instead of crossing an expensive school off your list, take your chances and apply for admission, as well as for financial aid. Most law schools will go out of their way to help you pay for the tuition if you take the time to fill out the right forms and meet the deadlines.

No matter which schools you apply to, be realistic about your expenses. The financial charges that each law school estimates are almost always a few hundred dollars under what you will actually need. Perhaps your meal contract costs a little more or your telephone bills weren't included. There's always some reason why you'll need to budget a little more money.

Where to Get Counseling

Relying on brochures and reputations is not sufficient if you really want to find the law school that will fit your needs. One of the best resources is your college's pre-law adviser. There is usually a dean or counselor in the career guidance office who has worked with pre-law students. This person can tell you about the individual law schools and about the types of students from your college who have attended those schools. Your adviser or dean can also help you decide what you want from a law school if you don't already know.

Another person who can give you advice on the various law schools is a current law student—someone who recently went through the selection process. If you are unable to visit law-school campuses and meet with students, you might visit your pre-law adviser and ask for a list of some students who are currently studying at some of the schools that interest you. Call the students and ask them some questions. Since they'd previously attended your college, they probably won't mind speaking with you. They are more likely to give you the inside information on each law school than the law school admissions office or an alumnus who graduated twenty-five years ago.

How Many Applications?

No matter what anyone tells you, don't think that you can get away with applying just to two or three law schools. Each school is looking for different types of applicants, so give yourself room for possible rejection. The best rule is to apply to at least seven law schools. You might want to include one or two schools that you are sure to be accepted by, judging by your academic records and their minimum requirements. And to round out your group of schools, you may also want to include one or two "reaching" schools—institutions which you would like to attend, but which ask for grades or scores that are higher than yours.

Law School Profiles

While it is difficult to say that a large law school is any better than a small one or that a private law school is better than a public one, there are definite advantages and disadvantages to attending each of them. The following profiles describe some of the characteristics of the different types of law schools.

Large State-Owned Law Schools

These schools can be located in urban or rural areas and usually offer a wide selection of courses. Although they generally attract first-rate professors, these schools have poor student–teacher ratios. There is not much personal contact with professors and it's difficult to get to know most fellow students on a personal level because there are so many of them. One definite advantage of attending these schools is that they are generally less expensive than other schools.

Small Private Law Schools

These schools are most often located in suburban areas and offer good student–teacher ratios. While the level of teaching is quite high if it is a quality school, there is rarely a great variety of second- and third-year electives offered. If the school is not well known there may be some problems when you go looking for a job. Perhaps employers aren't familiar with the school, or maybe only a few recruiters visit the campus. One obvious advantage here, though, is that competition is usually not so fierce when it comes to making Law Review and other journals.

Large Private Law Schools

Since being large and private is no guarantee of quality, be aware that there are large, private law schools that may not provide what you're looking for in a law school. One particular advantage to these schools is that, while they may be expensive, they often have large endowments and can afford to offer large scholarships to accepted students. Another benefit is that they are generally popular with job recruiters, so getting interviews may be easier when the time comes.

A disadvantage of many of these schools is that they are tremendously competitive—because of rigorous academic standards, the higher cost of tuition, and the size of the student body, students at these schools are often subject to enormous pressure.

You will be spending three strenuous years at the law school you choose to attend, so consider carefully all the factors that will affect your day-to-day life. There is a range of law schools in each of these categories that should provide an appropriate setting for every student.

A Few Words to the Older Student

Many law schools have admitted a substantial percentage of students who do not belong to the traditional twenty-two-years-old-and-graduating-from-college group. These students, frequently twenty-five years old and older, have applied to law school after several years or more in the business or academic world.

You should realize that you will not be alone in your decision to enter law school "late"—hundreds of applicants each year bring their valuable experience, sincere commitment, and different backgrounds with them when they enter a first-year class of law students.

What sets the older student apart from other law students varies. You may not enjoy the same flexibility that younger students have—you may need to attend law school in the evening after working full time at your job during the day. You may be a parent with child-care responsibilities that curtail your class time.

Whatever your needs, there should be a law school to satisfy them. Many law schools have part-time programs that offer evening and weekend classes. While this is uncommon among the most prestigious schools, you should write to the law schools that interest you (see the appendix) and inquire about their part-time curriculum. If you are able to attend full time, you should use the same criteria as a younger student for choosing a law school.

The Older Student's Application

Applicants who have been out of college several years or more may worry about the law school application process, but, assuming you have at least a bachelor's degree, there are only a few things of which to take special note.

You will be using the same application forms as every other applicant, but you may need to make special provisions for your college transcripts, recommendation letters, and written essay. Since all colleges maintain a permanent transcript of grades for each of its students, whatever their dates of graduation, you should have no difficulty having your transcript forwarded to the law schools once you apply to the Law School Data Assembly Service. Just follow the directions provided in any law school catalog or on the LSAT application form. Since all applicants must take the LSAT, all transcripts are forwarded to the law schools in the same manner.

An area that needs special consideration from you is your letters of recommendation. Although most student applicants ask their current professors to write letters for them, this may not be very practical or relevant for you. If you've been out of college for more than three years, it may be a waste of time to start looking for your old professors. Not only is there a chance that they've retired or left the school, but they've possibly forgotten you. Instead of persuading a former professor to write a mediocre letter with a few vague remarks about your performance in class seven years ago, it's better to get letters of recommendation from a current employer, a person that you've worked with on some project, or even a friend who knows you well and who is articulate.

The only other aspect of the process that will differ for those applicants who have been out of college for an extended period is the essay that most law schools request in their applications. Instead of talking about your college experiences, talk about your work experiences, your family, your career interests and any other experiences that you think would be relevant to your application. Law schools look favorably on admitting students who are older than college seniors—they are more mature, and often more serious about their decision to attend law school.

Use the essay to explain what you've been doing out in the "real world"—and why it has led you to apply to law school.

Outside of these few things, the application process is the same as it would be for the graduating college student. If you have any special concerns, contact the law schools that interest you and speak with someone in the student affairs office.

Strategy #7

Making Your Applications and Essays Stand Out

One of the most important strategies this book teaches is how to make your applications and essays stand out in the crowd. It is not enough just to fill in the blanks or write a few careless paragraphs. You have to make your application appear different from anyone else's, so that the admissions people remember you. You should also realize that each of your applications will be different; some applications ask very specific questions while others pose very general, open-ended questions.

There are usually two parts to every application. We'll label them "the application questions" (the fill-in-the-blank questions) and "the essay." In the second half of this chapter, we'll talk about the essay in great detail. But before discussing the application questions, let's talk about the logistics of collecting the applications themselves.

Sending for Applications

Your junior year is a good time to write to the law schools and ask for a copy of the catalog and the application. This is recommended so that a student can learn, in advance, what each law school asks for before he or she finally applies for admission in the fall of the senior year.

The best time to send away for the applications you will actually use is during the summer before your senior year. (Although the applications don't change too much from one year to the next, the one that you received as a junior cannot be used by the following year's candidates.) Instead of typing out a formal letter to the admissions office, you can simply send a postcard of three or four lines that reads something like this:

> To the Admissions Office:
>
> I am going to be a senior at Ohio State University this fall and I am interested in applying to your law school. Please send a catalog, application, and financial aid information to the following address. Thank you.
>
> William Crawford
> 133 Milford Drive
> Hohenwald, TN 38221

It is not necessary for you to go into any more detail than this. You need not tell them about your grade point average or LSAT scores because there are no prescreening efforts at the law schools. You also don't need to send a self-addressed stamped envelope. It's all free for the asking.

Once you've sent the post cards to the various law schools (see appendix) during the summer before your senior year, you should start receiving some applications by early September. If you ask for them anytime before the summer, you're bound to be sent *last year's* applications.

It may be wise to write to at least twelve or thirteen law schools. It's dangerous to limit yourself to just five or six schools—even if you are at the top of your class. By late September, you should have received all of the application forms and catalogs. If some are still missing, don't write to the schools again. It takes too much time. Use the list of phone numbers in the appendix and call the admissions office directly.

Two Charts That Will Get You Organized

Before you pick up a pen or pencil, read through all of your applications. Make sure that all of the pages and forms are there. The last thing you want to do is discover two weeks before the deadline that the application is missing a page. You should also avoid starting to write before you've read through everything and understood what the school is asking for.

Application-Requirement Chart

School	Application Fee	Due Date	Recommendations	Essays	Transcripts	LSAT Scores
Southern Law	$25	Jan. 15	2 teachers	3	due Jan. 20	won't accept winter exam
Madison Law	$35	Feb. 1	1 teacher	optional	due Feb. 1	accepts winter exam
Carlisle Law	$30	Jan. 15	optional	1	due Feb. 1	accepts winter exam
Vernon Law	$30	Feb. 10	employer or teacher	1 formal 1 creative	due Feb. 10	accepts winter exam

What's-My-Progress Chart

School	Application	Essays	Recommendations	Contacts
Southern Law	finished	all 3 first drafts completed	have Prof. Jenkins's need Prof. Smith's	Uncle Fred is an alum.
Madison Law	need Mom and Dad's soc. sec. no.	use one from Southern Law	ask Dean Harrison	
Carlisle Law	ready to be typed	ask professor to read	photocopy Prof. Jenkins's letter	Prof. Smith knows admissions officer
Vernon Law	ask adviser about question no. 6b	both typed and ready	remind Mrs. Black at City Hall	Jeff P. is on law review

It will make your life easier if you draw up a chart that is similar to the following one. This "Application-Requirement Chart" will help you place all the information about your applications on one sheet of paper. It's not enough to answer some questions and write a few essays—you have to keep up with deadlines for recommendations, transcripts, test scores, as well as various fees that have to be paid. This organization chart can be used for the entire process, to remind you when to take care of each item. If there are any additional concerns that your applications pose, allow space for them in your chart. Don't clutter your memory with details when you can write them down and have them at your fingertips.

Once your chart is completed, you should photocopy each page of every application form. While it will cost you a few dollars, it's well worth it. Many students make the mistake of putting pen to paper the very minute that they receive the application. Since law schools are looking for flawless applications (without cross outs, typing mistakes, or grammatical errors), it's best to do the first draft on the photocopies.

It might be a good idea to draw up another chart now, which you can use later to record your own progess with the application procedure. While the "Application-Requirement Chart" tells you what each of the law schools wants from you, the "What's-My-Progress Chart" lets you keep track of how, if, and when you've satisfied those requirements. It's a place where you can jot down the specifics of what you want to include in the essay, whom you've asked to write the recommendations, what's been completed, what needs more work, and so forth.

The Application Questions

The first half of the law-school application is fairly simple. Questions will deal with topics ranging from your social security number to your grade point average and your LSAT score. Since you're working on a photocopy now, don't worry about mistakes.

While you will probably have no difficulty with this section, there are certain questions that you should pay particular attention to. On the application, you will be asked to list your high school, your college, and your estimated rank in class. If you have a rank, list it. If you have a very low rank and are afraid that it might turn off the admissions people before they get to see the rest of your application, you may want to leave it out.

Some law schools demand that you list all your "numbers" (grades, scores) right on the first page of the application. This can be a real disadvantage if you don't have outstanding, eye-catching numbers. Even if you have great activities and work experience, they won't see that until the second page. Yale Law School has an application like this. Usually their second question asks for your LSAT scores, and if that's not being forward enough, they go on to ask what you scored on the SAT in high school! Do you even remember that score?

Another question you will often be asked is whether or not you have received any academic honors. This means you should list special scholastic prizes, dean's list, Phi Beta Kappa, cum laude, and so forth. If you've received some of these distinctions, list all of them. If your school doesn't give awards like dean's list or other prizes, let the law school know that. Instead of leaving that obvious blank space, say something. Blank spaces frequently speak louder than your answers, so cover yourself.

You will also be asked about your extracurricular activities. Some schools will tell you to list just three or four, and they will only leave about two or three lines of space for you to discuss them. If this is your strong area, then play it up for all it's worth. Attach an additional page and explain in detail why your activities are important, how many hours you spend on them, what you've achieved through them, and anything else that might impress the reader of your application.

Most law schools will ask about your summer jobs or term-time employment on campus. No matter how professional your job was, list it. On-campus employment is particularly important; it can help explain any low grades if you've had to work long hours to pay for your tuition.

Questions Not to Answer

Sometimes you may be faced with a question that you simply don't want to answer. Whether you have an answer for it or not, a law school might pose a question that you feel is unfair. An example of this might be a question that asks you to list all the other law schools that interest you. There's no advantage to telling Jacksonville School of Law that you're applying to Harvard, Duke, Berkeley, and Yale Law Schools.

You also may be asked if you have any illnesses or handicaps that may impair your ability to perform well in law school. The only right answer here is "no." If you write anything else, the school is bound to look at you as a liability. A "yes" will require you to give all sorts of explanations and excuses that will potentially weaken your case. If you want to go to that law school (with a handicap or not), it should be your own decision. The only handicaps that you might want to notify them about after acceptance are those for which they might need to make special arrangements (for example, a dormitory room on the ground floor if you are in a wheelchair).

Advantage Questions

On your application, you may see questions that can work to your advantage. One of these might be a request for you to list any friends or relatives who have attended the law school. Do your best with this. Whether it's a parent, next-door neighbor, or just a person you know casually, the alumni connection may help. If you happen to be applying to Cornell Law School and your former music teacher was a member of the Cornell family, let the admissions people know. If you work at it, you may find a connection to every school.

Another question that may be asked of you is whether you belong to a minority group or have any special background that might distinguish you from other applicants. Let the school know if you are an American Indian or a member of another group which has poor representation in the law schools. Even if you have an outstanding academic record, you will be given additional consideration by the admissions people.

Shortcuts

Since applications can be tedious and time consuming, it's a good idea to use shortcuts whenever you can. One of the best ways to save time is by going through all of your applications, circling the questions that you can't answer, and then listing them separately. Because some of these questions might require you to contact your parents, the dean, or the registrar, do it all at once.

Another place to save time on the applications is on your essays. You will find that many schools will ask you to write an essay on the same topic.

The Essay

Almost every law school will ask you to write a short essay. You may be given specific directions to keep it to one thousand words or even one typed page. These essays are extremely important, and they should not be written hurriedly. Not only will the essay provide a chance for you to give more details about your achievements that might impress the law school, but it will also help the admissions people to get to know you as an individual.

While some essay questions will be vague and simply ask you to write about yourself, most will ask special questions like: What have you done that makes you unusual? Why do you want to attend law school or become a lawyer? What are some of your most significant experiences? These are all personal questions which take time to answer. You want to make sure that not only are you sincere in your answers, but that you provide information that further enhances your application. Many students structure their essays in order to mention as many of their special experiences and activities as possible, while also showing how their strongest personal qualities have developed through those experiences.

If you are a creative person, you may want to write about a particularly unusual topic which displays an aspect of your personality. When the questions are not very specific, you may write whatever you like.

Sample Essays

In this section, we will be looking at one law school candidate and the three forms in which his essay might have been written. Phrasing is extremely important, and you should study the three sample essays that Roger, a student who was applying to Northwest Law School, might have written. Although each essay says much the same thing, each is written in a different style. The first is the "uptight, overkill essay," the second is the "overly casual, honest, and modest essay," and the third is the "right-on-target essay."

The Uptight, Overkill Essay

There is one sure way to turn off an admissions officer, and that is to come across as being too aggressive or abrasive. It's nice to highlight your strengths, but it is tactless to pat yourself on the back constantly as Roger did in this first essay.

The essay question that Roger was given was: "Please tell in a five-hundred-word essay, how your experiences, education, or other background have led you to apply to our law school." In the first version of his essay, Roger comes across as too aggressive. As you can see, he appears pompous and too self-assured, beginning almost every sentence with "I" or "my." Here, Roger almost seems to flaunt his accomplishments. He makes the mistake of comparing himself to other students only to say, "I am better!", commenting that "other students were doing menial labor at fast-food restaurants," while he had a job in a fancy law office. Roger gets three big strikes for snobbery, immaturity, and narrow-mindedness.

This essay is just too pushy. Roger hammers the reader over the head by stating every one of his good qualities: "I am trustworthy, loyal, helpful . . ." After insisting pointedly that he cares about "all the poor people," Roger then mentions all the wealthy lawyers who belong to his country club.

Roger probably meant no harm. He simply wanted to emphasize his background and experiences. His mistake was in not looking at his essay objectively. He comes across as unpleasant and too self-important. Look at this first essay closely, and make sure you don't make the same mistakes.

I am applying to you now because as far back as I can remember, I have wanted to study under the fine professors at Northwest Law School. All my life I have wanted to be the best—and attending your school will allow me to continue that tradition. I have always selected or been introduced to experiences that have brought me closer to my goal of becoming one of the ten best lawyers in our country. Going to Northwest would certainly be the icing on the cake.

I will now explain specifically how my background has brought me to the point of applying to your law school:

I have spent a great deal of time around lawyers, ever since my summer internship before freshman year at the law firm of Knox, Mudd, Rose and Bush. While I was involved in serious projects with these top Denver attorneys, other students my age were doing menial labor at fast-food restaurants or summer day camps. I obviously had the foresight to learn about the legal profession very early in life.

My involvement in the Boy Scouts also exemplifies many of the qualities that one would find in a lawyer. The fact that I reached the level of Life Scout (one step below the top), shows that I have a talent for getting along with others and an interest in facing challenging experiences. Being a Boy Scout also taught me all the qualities and morals that a lawyer needs to know. I am trustworthy, loyal, helpful, friendly, courteous, kind, cheerful—and all the other things that a good Scout would be. Because of this background, I also understand the importance of community service—and I know that your school encourages this through its clinical programs to aid the poor in housing problems. Boy Scouts taught me to care about all the poor people.

My family's membership at the Seacrest Country Club has also played a role in my choice to attend a top law school like yours. In addition to being in the company of the wealthiest lawyers in Denver, my activities at the Club include being Chairman of the Youth Advisory Committee. I have given great leadership to this eighteen-member group (between the ages of fifteen and twenty-one). Leadership is an important quality that I know your law school must be looking for in students.

> I have served as president of the freshman class, sophomore class, and senior class at Westlake College, which not only shows my interest in governing others, but also underscores the fact that I am well-respected by my classmates. I know that being liked by others is one of my . . .

The Overly Casual, Honest, and Modest Essay

Just as you can be too pompous in an essay, you can also be too modest. Failing to make the most of your good qualities and your accomplishments can do just as much damage as bragging. Remember that modesty is not going to get you anywhere in the application process. The students who are competing against you for space in law school classes are an assertive, ambitious group. If you do what Roger did in this second version of his essay, you will suffer in comparison with your peers.

This second essay seems to be the polar opposite of the first one. While the first essay portrayed an aggressive person, this one describes a timid, unsure applicant. Here, Roger refers to himself as "ordinary" and as having potential to become a "fairly good lawyer." His lack of confidence is very unappealing. Roger's further effort to be absolutely honest doesn't help him either. There is no reason to say that his father got him his summer job, or that he was bored by his law-office experience. It's doubtful that these comments will impress admissions people.

You should also notice the casual tone that Roger uses in this essay. His writing would not convince any reader that he has developed a mature style. Try to use a bit of formality in your essays.

> Although none of my experiences are particularly interesting or unusual, I have come to the conclusion that I might make a fairly good lawyer. Since Northwest has a curriculum that fits my needs, it is one of the nine law schools that I am applying to now.
>
> My background is quite ordinary, and as you can see from my transcript, I graduated from a typical upper-middle class high school before attending Westlake College. Though Westlake was a good school and although I maintained a decent average, I really never decided to consider law school until it dawned on me that I had nothing else to do after college.

After my father helped me get a job with a medium-size Denver law firm, I had my first introduction to the business. What had originally turned me off about the place was how many hours people worked. While I can work hard for grades, I have to be honest and say that I'd lose my mind if I had to sit in one place for three hours. In the office, I did filing, photocopying, and some other office chores.

Once I followed my brother into the Boy Scouts, I really found something that I liked. I like nothing better than getting outside in the fresh air. Being cooped up in a classroom or building all day is the pits—unless, of course, you're getting paid for it! After two more years in the Scout troop I quit at the rank of Life Scout. Since I like facing new experiences, it served its purpose. I made lots of friends and we all had a great time.

Outside of the things that I already mentioned, a group of guys from my neighborhood and I are really involved at our Country Club. Although my parents originally joined it in order to make good contacts for me and for their own careers, I found that the Youth Advisory Committee was doing some interesting things. Because of the group, we've gotten the club to do things for the younger members.

Like many colleges, Westlake happens to have an apathetic student body. Hardly anybody there gets involved in school government, so I ended up being president of the class—three times! I ran unopposed the first two times and then got drafted the last time (this year). Although I became senior class president by accident, it has taught me a lot of things that a lawyer should probably know when . . .

The Right-on-Target Essay

Now that you've seen the wrong versions of Roger's essay, the following is the correct version. You will notice that it makes the most of each activity without using a pompous tone. This essay was well planned, and very carefully explains why Roger wants to become a lawyer, and why he wants to attend Northwest.

Most of the facts used in this essay were mentioned in the first two versions. The major difference is the tone. This essay portrays a confident person who is not only talented, but who is also sympathetic to others. Read the essay closely and see if your own background can be conveyed in an equally appealing form.

Our education and our life experiences play a major role in the choices that we ultimately make. Looking back on the past few years of my life, I can clearly see how I became interested in the legal profession and why I decided to apply to Northwest Law School. Before going into greater detail about how my past activities and education fit into my future as a lawyer, let me tell you why I am attracted to Northwest.

While almost every comment that I've heard about Northwest has been positive, I have been the most impressed with what people have said about your courses and professors that deal with civil rights law—an area that I would especially like to pursue.

From my very first summer job in the law firm of Knox, Mudd, Rose and Bush, I realized that I wanted to be a lawyer. But what was so odd about my decision was that it was not based on the fact that I wanted to do what the lawyers in this Denver corporate law firm were doing. I made my decision on the basis of what this firm was *not* doing.

Although I have the utmost respect for the attorneys there, I realized that all their clients were big U.S. corporations and other wealthy businesses abroad. I asked myself, "Are there any good firms that help the less wealthy and the other underprivileged?" I knew that not everyone could afford the rates that Knox, Mudd charged.

Becoming involved with the Boy Scouts and the community service functions that we performed brought me even closer to my decision to investigate civil rights law. Because of the values that are taught by the Boy Scouts, I learned the importance of being loyal and being a friend to those whom I hardly knew. When one grows up in a fairly well-off suburb, it's easy to become isolated and not befriend people from different backgrounds. Staying in the Boy Scouts until I reached the second highest rank (Life Scout), I tried to learn all that it had to offer.

What was perhaps the final experience that reaffirmed my decision to become a civil-rights lawyer and to look at Northwest's strong curriculum in that area was my family's unfortunate membership in the Seacrest Country Club. I say "unfortunate" because we became aware that it practiced blatant discrimination against different ethnic groups. Although I had been in the important leadership position as Chairperson of the eighteen-member Youth Advisory Committee, I had been unaware that my own club was racist. Even though it's a private organization, I feel this is unacceptable policy.

Because of my interest in civil rights, I have tried to make some changes at Westlake. As class president for three years, I have . . .

Strategy #8

Using Recommendations and Contacts to Your Advantage

As you probably realize by now, the law school admissions process is very similar to the college admissions process. Just as colleges required you to take an entrance exam and prepare written essays, so do the law schools. Another aspect that the law schools share with the colleges is their desire to see what others think of you. The way most admissions people satisfy this need is by asking for at least one or two letters of recommendation.

The reason a letter of recommendation is especially important in the selection process is that it provides information about you that the admissions people generally can't find in your essay or your grade point average. And since there are generally no personal interviews granted by law schools, their only way to judge you is through the comments of those who are asked to recommend you.

The Purpose of a Recommendation Letter

When law schools are selecting students, they have to look beyond the college transcript and beyond your list of extracurricular activities. The schools are not just selecting students who can score well on exams or win prestigious awards; they are looking for students who display enthusiasm, integrity, and a willingness to work with others. These qualities are not only found in the student who has an A average or who ranks in the LSAT's ninety-ninth percentile.

Because law schools want to find out what the applicants are like personally, they ask you for recommendations from professors, deans, or employers who have had a chance to observe your work, your attitude, your motivation, and your integrity. While many undergraduate colleges requested recommendation letters as a way of collecting information to supplement your performance in a personal interview, law schools must rely much more heavily on these letters. It is for this reason that you must take the request for recommendations very seriously.

Whom to Ask for Recommendations

Although most law schools will ask you to provide one or two professor recommendations, you should do this even for the law schools that fail to request such letters. Assuming that the letter would be positive, it can only be to your advantage to have someone write one for you.

Now, whom do you ask? Besides providing each school with one or two teacher recommendations, there are many other people who can write supplementary letters. Here's a list of possibilities:

- summer job employers
- deans or other college administrators
- business people who know you personally
- minister or rabbi
- a sports coach or adviser to one of your activities
- a roommate or close friend
- any alumnus whom you have met or worked with

No matter whom you ask to recommend you, always make sure that the writer likes you and knows you well enough to write a personal letter that not only gives facts, but also conveys the positive aspects of your personality. Avoid selecting a person simply because he or she has an impressive title. If you're not careful, you can end up with a letter that can actually hurt your chances for acceptance. Later in this chapter, you'll see some sample letters and discover how and why some of the worst ones were written by prominent individuals.

How to Ask and How Many to Ask For

The first rule when collecting letters of recommendation is never to wait until your applications are almost due. Many students wait until three weeks before the deadline to ask a professor or other person to write a letter. If you give someone such short notice, the person will either refuse to do it, or just scribble a shoddy paragraph or two of unimpressive comments.

A good idea is to collect one or two recommendations at the end of each semester of college—and to start this long before you begin the application process. When Michael, a sophomore, decided that he would eventually apply to law school, he approached his favorite professors at the end of the fall semester and later the spring semester, and asked them to write a two- or three-paragraph letter on his behalf. Michael then had each professor place the individual letters on file in the career placement office or in their respective departmental offices. (Some college deans' offices offer this service as well.) At the end of each of his junior-year semesters, Michael asked a few more professors to write for him.

By the time he began his senior year, Michael had already collected six recommendations. And what was so terrific about his system was that since he had approached his writers within a few weeks after classes ended, they had no difficulty remembering him and his best personal qualities when they wrote the letters.

While many law schools provide special forms for your recommendations, some will simply ask you to have someone write, on a separate sheet, about your personality, integrity, and potential as a law student. It's a good idea simply to ask your reference to use his or her office stationery and to type a two- or three-paragraph letter that can later be photocopied for each of your schools. This saves your professor from having to type ten different copies for each of your ten different law schools.

Making It Easy for the Letter Writer

In order to get the very best recommendation, make it easy for your writer. Don't assume anything. Don't assume that he remembers all your activities. Don't assume that she's written dozens of letters in the past. Don't assume that he will remember when and where to mail your letter. And finally, don't assume that she'll want to spend money for the envelope and postage.

You can make it easy for your reference by giving the person a copy of your resume or some other listing of your achievements, activities, and hobbies. Also on this sheet, list any specific career interests so that they can be mentioned in the letter. On the top of the page, list the date that the recommendation should be mailed. If you list the day that it's due, the professor will inevitably wait until that day to mail it.

Sitting down with the reference for a few minutes, politely suggest that you would like the letter to be approximately two or three paragraphs, and that it should be typed so it can later be photocopied. Providing an addressed and stamped envelope will save your reference from having to shell out extra money or remember addresses. A week before the recommendation should be mailed, call the writer and say thank you. This will not only show your appreciation, but will serve as a reminder to complete the mission if it hasn't already been done.

How to Screen the Recommendations

Since most law schools ask that your letters be sent directly from the reference to the dean or pre-law adviser, you will never see them. And although some professors will give you a copy of their letters, most will not. One way to make sure that a poor or mediocre recommendation is not forwarded by the pre-law adviser or dean is to ask him or her to select the two or three best letters from your file. This is why it is important to have at least four different letters to choose from.

Another method that some students use to screen their recommendations is not a very ethical one. Whether you do it or not is your own business, but if you get caught, be prepared to face the consequences. When Rena was applying to law schools, she knew that she had five letters on file with the pre-law adviser. Knowing that she was supposed to provide preaddressed envelopes for the adviser to place the letters in and then seal tightly so that she could enclose them (unopened) with her application, Rena thought of a way that she could get to unseal the envelopes and read the confidential letters. Here's how she did it:

Though she knew she was only applying to seven schools, Rena gave an eighth envelope (for an eighth law school) to her pre-law adviser and he sealed all five of her recommendation letters in it, telling her that she was to enclose the sealed envelope with the rest of her application. Rena dashed back to her dormitory, opened the envelope of recommendations, and read each one. Since there was no eighth law school, she didn't have to mail this envelope full of letters anyway. Realize that if you do this, you're starting your legal career with a mark against your integrity. It's your decision.

Alumni Contacts

Another powerful force in your recommendation file can be letters written by law-school alumni. Though these should never be used in lieu of teacher recommendations, they can always add weight to your application if they are well written and if the writer is an alumnus, especially one who contributes generously to the particular school. If the alumnus is actively involved with the law school, he may offer to phone the admissions office. Accept the offer, but politely ask him to send a letter too. While a call is more direct, a letter is a permanent record.

A Bad Letter Versus a Mediocre Letter Versus a Good Letter

Now that we've talked about whom and when to ask for recommendation letters, let's look at some sample letters and see how three different students elicited different types of comments.

How to Get a Bad Letter of Recommendation

Each year, there are students who end up being rejected on the basis of a bad letter of recommendation. How can someone get a bad recommendation? There are many ways to elicit a negative letter from a reference. Here are four of them:

- Ask a professor who does not like you personally.
- Persuade an unwilling person to write for you.
- Insist that the reference mention certain things in his or her letter.
- Ask someone who has no respect for you or your achievements.

As ridiculous as it seems, there are students who make all four of the above mistakes when they choose their letter writers. And what do they end up with? They receive tersely written notes or blatantly negative letters. Professors and other references are human, and just because they are mature professionals doesn't mean that all of them are adult enough to hide their animosities. No matter how they behave in the classroom, if they don't *want* to recommend you, they will write a bad letter. While some will tell you openly that they cannot write a positive recommendation, others will agree to write a letter and weaken your chances for admission.

When Joy Armstrong, a student at a state university, applied for law school, she went to one of her school's most prominent professors. Not only was he a busy man, but he didn't particularly care for Joy's abrasive personality. When she asked him to recommend her, he snapped, "Can't you ask some *other* professor?" Although Joy should have taken this as a hint, she insisted that he write for her. She was determined that he do it since she had gotten an A in his class and since he was well known in his field. She then presented the annoyed professor with a list of achievements that he should mention in the letter. Here is what resulted:

To the Admissions Office:

I am writing this letter on behalf of Joy Armstrong, who is applying to your law school. Joy was one of my students in *The Modern Novel* last semester and received an A in the class.

Joy wanted me to write and tell you what a diligent worker she is and what a competent lawyer she would make. I can honestly say that Joy is indeed a diligent worker, and if her ambition, cool determination, and ability to get what she goes after is any sign of her competence as a future lawyer, then she will certainly be successful.

Joy suggested I mention how wonderfully she has run the school newspaper as managing editor. While I've no clue about her ability to direct or get along with others on the paper's staff, I can attest to the fact that she is bold enough to tell her professors what grades to give her (as she once did with me). Joy Armstrong is not a shy person, and I have absolute faith that she will brazenly face any problem with her typical Armstrong zeal and forcefulness that we at Rockland State College have come to know.

Another point that Joy said I should stress to you was her concern for those around her. Although she might first appear to be a materialistic person, Miss Armstrong got the opportunity to showcase her generosity as director of the university blood donor drive and as a volunteer during a three-month stint at a local nursing home. The entire university community became aware of her charity after Joy utilized her public relations prowess and staged the first press conference in the nursing home's twenty-eight year history.

I recommend Joy to you because she possesses all the aggressive qualities that, no doubt, can be useful to an ambitious lawyer.

Sincerely,

This is clearly a negative letter which did not aid Joy's candidacy for law school. But since the student never knew what her professor wrote, she assumed that it was a positive account of her class performance and personality.

In looking at the recommendation, one can see that while there are no blatant criticisms of the candidate, each paragraph includes at least one or two subtly phrased undercuts. Each of the three main paragraphs begins with a statement that lets the reader know that Joy "forced" him to say this. The professor uses the phrases: "Joy wanted me to write . . ." "Joy told me to say . . ." "Joy said I should stress . . ." The law school can see that this person is reluctantly repeating the applicant's claims. Also evident in this letter is the writer's perception of the candidate as an overly ambitious student. Joy should have known her reference sufficiently to realize that he thought she was "aggressive," "materialistic," and self-serving enough to call attention to her volunteerism with a PR gimmick. The fact that he was a prominent professor did her no service.

And while you may laugh, this can happen to anyone. If a reference has a chance to be honest, dislikes you, and knows you'll never see the letter, you may end up with a real strike against you in your personal file.

How to Get a Mediocre Letter of Recommendation

The second type of recommendation that we will look at is one that stands somewhere between a negative letter and a positive endorsement of an applicant. These mediocre or wishy-washy letters are perhaps the most common form of recommendation. Although they rarely speak against the student, they are no help either. Following are some of the situations in which a student may elicit a mediocre recommendation.

- Ask a professor who gave you an average grade (B or less).
- Approach a teacher whom you haven't seen in three years or more.
- Choose a reference who is not very articulate.
- Ask a professor with whom you've never spent a private moment (outside of the classroom).

When Ted, a college senior, began his quest for law-school recommendations, he managed to elicit the following mediocre letter. Not only did he ask a teacher who had given him a B, but it was a teacher whom he hadn't seen since the course had ended—three years earlier! It also appears that the professor had forgotten just about every significant detail about the student. The law school can see that while the writer is articulate, he is at a loss for comments. He can only note grade averages and a few factual pieces of information about the student's background.

> To the Admissions Office:
>
> I am writing on behalf of Ted Osborn, a former student of mine at Greenvale University. Ted was in my introductory biology class three years ago and received a B.

Ted is a congenial person who remains active in several sports, including swimming and basketball. While I don't recall him being one of my top students, I am sure that he worked hard in the class. Ted comes from a very small town in Indiana where both of his parents are practicing attorneys. He said that this was one of his primary reasons for choosing law school.

Although I haven't seen Ted during the last two years and can't recall any specific projects that he presented in our introductory seminar (each student was required to present three projects), I have his grades listed as B-plus, B, and B-plus. He had received a B for his class participation, but he appears to have become much more outspoken because he's now a vice-president of the senior class.

While Ted was not an unusual student by any means, I don't ever recall having any real problems with him. I don't remember having to discipline him, as I often find myself doing with freshmen and sophomores. And now, three years later, I feel he has come quite a ways. I am glad he remembered me and asked that I recommend him because I feel he will probably be a good asset to your law school.

Sincerely,

While it's not a bad letter, the above recommendation lacks the exuberance that an admissions officer is looking for in an appraisal of a student. There are no remarks in the letter that characterize the applicant in a special light. And because the letter sounds ordinary, the student appears ordinary.

Throughout the letter, there are remarks like "While I don't recall . . ." and "I don't remember . . ." These phrases tell the admissions people that the writer is not giving an accurate record of the applicant either because the student failed to leave an impression or simply because so much time has passed.

Ted was principally at fault here because he approached a teacher who hadn't worked with him in three years. How on earth is a teacher going to remember your special attributes if you've let this much time slip by? In order to prevent this, a student should either have the professor write a recommendation as soon as the semester ends and put it on file, or else just approach professors from junior and senior year classes. Reaching back to a freshman year teacher can hurt you if you failed to leave a lasting impression.

Another common reason for the mediocre letter is that it is written by a professor who doesn't feel you are an outstanding student. It makes good sense to overlook the professor who gave you less than a B-plus. If you received a B-minus in his course, it's difficult for the professor to say you were outstanding—even if you *did* work hard for the grade.

How to Get a Positive Letter of Recommendation

If you've followed the advice in this chapter, you will be able to elicit a positive letter from each of your references. While it may take a little more time to find the best people, it will make a difference in the long run.

When Donna, an outstanding pre-law student, collected her letters, she took note of the following hints.

- Only accept a recommendation from someone who is enthusiastic about writing for you.
- Ask a professor who knows about your classroom performance *and* your extracurricular activities.
- Choose a writer who thinks you are either equal to his best students or superior to them.
- Ask a person who honestly believes you would make a good lawyer.

Here is a good example of a positive recommendation:

To the Admissions Office:

I am extremely happy to write to you on behalf of Donna Fagenson, a student who is applying to your law school this year. Donna was a student with whom I worked very closely in my Soviet Politics seminar. I am also in the position to make a recommendation in my capacity as adviser to Donna's thesis project.

Donna Fagenson is one of the most committed students that I have had in recent years at Bridgehampton College. Not only was she always well prepared and enthusiastic when she arrived in class, but she undertook a very unusual midterm presentation for which she received an A. In my class, Soviet Politics 250, I give students the option to write a paper or present a "creative project" for their midterm grade. While most students chose the traditional research paper, Donna chose to present a project.

Utilizing her creativity and a great deal of time, Donna chose to take a classwide poll of students' knowledge and attitudes concerning Soviet Politics. After doing her own research on the Soviet Union, she compared the real facts with the assumptions that students had always *considered* as fact. Combining library research, extensive polling, and a wonderful oral presentation, Donna put together a terrifically interesting project. This is all to say that she is not only enthusiastic and hard working, but she is also creative and eager to take on unusual demands. She has an especially analytic mind, as I often noticed in our class discussions.

While working with Miss Fagenson on her thesis project, I had the chance to see another side of her. Because we often met in the student lounge, I had the chance to see how she performed outside of the classroom. Whenever we were there, she was always approached by classmates who wanted to say "hello." She appears to get along with students from every background. I honestly believe that Donna represents all of the positive academic and personal qualities that you are looking for in a student. She should do well in the legal field.

Sincerely,

It certainly must be obvious to you why this letter is better than the first two. Not only does it speak positively about the student (there are no phrases with "maybe," "perhaps," "I don't remember"), it is obvious that Donna held the respect of her professor. What also makes this letter special is that it comments on a specific project that Donna performed, while also highlighting her personal qualities. When a reference can be this specific as well as enthusiastic, the admissions people will be certain to remember the applicant. This is the kind of letter that you want, so try to find a person who is likely to write such a recommendation.

Strategy #9

Dealing with Parents

Even if you're living on a college campus three hundred miles from home, you may still feel pressure from your parents during the law school application process. What you need to understand is how your parents must feel during this time. Not only do *you* face the daily worry of being rejected, so do they.

What makes it even more difficult for most parents is that they don't understand how the application or selection process actually works. There's a way to make it easier on their nerves, and a way to keep them from making weekly phone calls that begin with "Have you heard yet?" Sit down and explain to your parents that there are many components to your application: your grades, LSAT score, application, essay and letters of recommendation. Most parents feel that the ultimate decision is under your direct control (so if you get the application finished earlier than everyone else, you'll get in).

Explain to them that most law schools do not respond to students until April. This will keep them from phoning you each evening to ask if any reply has been received. Parents often have a knack for getting their kids nervous when there is really nothing to worry about, but as long as they feel they're being informed about everything and as long as they have faith that you're sending the right forms in on time, they'll leave you alone.

But then there's that special parent. While few of us like to admit it, there are mothers and fathers who are not so easy to satisfy. These parent-types can be a nuisance, but fortunately there's a way to deal with them.

The Let-Me-Check-Over-All-Your-Applications-Before-Mailing Parent

Although this parent gives you the impression that he doesn't think you're capable of completing a positive application by yourself, don't let him offend you. Tell him that you appreciate his concern, but that it is against the rules for anyone except the student to work on the application. If he insists, send him a photocopy and tell him that you will consider all of his corrections. Having a parent like this isn't all bad—at least he can catch your spelling mistakes.

The Don't-Apply-Because-We-Can't-Afford-Law-School Parent

In many ways, this parent is trying to act in your best interest. He doesn't want you to apply and then get your hopes up when he can't afford to send you to the law school. Be gentle with the parent who asks you not to apply because of financial reasons, but explain that all of your law schools give financial aid to those who need it. Tell him that you would not attend a school that will not help you find a sufficient number of grants and loans.

The You-Must-Go-to-Law-School-Whether-You-Like-It-or-Not Parent

This can be the most damaging parent, and you have to handle him firmly. If you have no desire to become a lawyer, you're wasting your time going through the application process. There are definitely parents who try to shove a professional career down their children's throats, and this can be quite damaging. Try to reason with your parents and explain that they will be wasting their money on something you don't want. Most parents will back down when you tell them that law school can be a $50,000 investment.

If the money doesn't matter to your parents and they use threats to get you to apply (don't laugh—there are parents who do this), you could go through the motions, doing a sloppy job with everything (the LSAT, applications, and so forth) in order to make sure you get rejected. If it's the only way out, then it may be worth it.

The You-Haven't-Got-a-Snowball's-Chance Parent

Then there are the parents who are totally unsupportive. Pay them no mind. They may be displaying this attitude in order to prepare themselves for a rejection, or (more likely) because they are slyly trying to motivate you. If a parent tells a child that he'll never be able to do something, the child usually tries twice as hard to accomplish the challenging project. Tell this person that you disagree with him, and that you'll need his help to prove him wrong.

The Alma Mater Parent

Whether it's by coincidence or by design, there happen to be a large number of law school applicants who are the sons or daughters of attorneys. While you may resist applying to your parents' alma mater, you will be making a foolish mistake—no matter how much of an "individual" you would like to be.

There is a definite advantage if your parents are alumni of the law school. Many schools ask you specifically, on the application, if you have a relative who attended their school. It will always help you if a close relation is an alumna or alumnus, whether he or she donates money or not.

How Parents Can Help

While it's wrong to let your parents write your essays or fill out your applications, there are many ways that they can aid you in the law school application process. You can use your parents as sounding boards as you write your essay. Ask them if it sounds too pompous or too modest. Get them to read the application and to look for spelling mistakes. They'll enjoy doing this because they'll feel that they are contributing.

Parents can also help by introducing you to any co-workers or friends who might have attended law school. These people can give you career advice.

Any method that you use to involve your parents is a welcome one. Whether by making a creative suggestion on how to portray yourself better in an essay, or correcting your grammar on the application, many parents want to contribute—so let them.

Strategy #10

Ten Mistakes to Avoid While Applying

No matter how many rules you've been given in this book or at the pre-law adviser's office, it's impossible to remember everything. For this reason, this strategy will give you the ten most important points to keep in mind. This strategy warns you against the ten most common and most detrimental mistakes that the law school applicant can make. If you forget everything else that you've learned about the application process, at least remember to avoid doing the following:

1. *Lying or stretching the truth in an application.*
   As warned earlier in this book, liars are usually caught. No matter how much it appears to improve your record, misrepresenting activities or other achievements can ruin your chances of admission if anyone suspects you. It's a small world and you'd be surprised how many admissions officers know your deans, fellow classmates, and professors. Also remember that if one school catches you in a lie, they'll make a serious effort to contact another. It's hard to erase a bad reputation—and that's very important to a future lawyer.

2. *Letting fellow classmates look at your completed application.*
   If you don't already know what the word *anxiety* means, you'll be certain to learn by the time this whole application process ends. Much of the tension exists not only because your classmates are discussing their applications, but also because they are all competing against each other. Many people, including your roommates and best friends, may ask to look at your application. Whether they want to give advice, check for errors,

or simply see how you've portrayed yourself, don't show the application to them. Not that you're being paranoid, but if you've spent hours creating an original essay, you don't want another applicant (friend or not) to borrow the idea.

3. *Nagging the admissions office to grant you a personal interview.*

You will not only waste your own time trying to convince the admissions people to interview you, but you will waste their time. And rest assured, they remember anyone who tries to infringe on their time and their rules. There *are* informational interviews at some schools, but it is next to impossible to receive an evaluative interview unless your uncle happens to be dean of the law school (and even then, your chances are slim). If you nag the admissions office, someone may just take it out on you when your application comes up for discussion. Remember, they're only human.

4. *Taking the LSAT without preparing for it.*

Although not everyone takes a review course or buys a study manual, only a fool would walk into this four-hour exam without becoming familiar with the format and the directions. Not only does this test force you to work under pressure, but it also demands that you use skills that are not always important for other exams. It is no simple quiz that measures natural intelligence—it is a difficult six-part test with an additional essay question.

5. *Calling the admissions office before the notification date and asking them if you've gotten in yet.*

Once again, we're back to nagging the admissions office. Making a bad name for yourself with these people can only mean trouble. Of course, the temptation to call is great, especially when friends have already heard from the school. But the thing to keep in mind is that if you haven't been rejected yet, just be grateful. Some law schools will send letters to the "definite rejects" very early. Other schools have a specific notification date (often in late March) and will not tell you anything until that day has arrived.

6. *Being too creative in your application and essay.*

Gourmet angel food cakes. Essays written in pig Latin. Hybrid rose bushes. These are all things that you should not send with your application. You want to stand out and be noticed, but being too creative can work against your chances of admission. While it's important to stress (and perhaps show reasonable samples of) your talents, personal qualities, and special interests, you don't want to portray yourself as an oddball. Turning yourself into a spectacle is generally not to your advantage. While some lawyers have begun to advertise their rates on television, as a group they are generally conservative. Most admissions people aim to keep it that way.

7. *Waiting until the last minute to collect letters of recommendation.*

Procrastinating is something that comes easy to all of us. Unfortunately, so will bad recommendations if you're not careful. Since law-school recommendations are essentially a substitute for personal interviews, you must do everything you can to elicit positive, well-written letters. The secret to doing this is making good use of time in every possible way. Give people at least two to three weeks to write a letter. If they feel rushed, it will be detected in the tone and quality of their writing.

8. *Being too modest about your achievements.*

This is one of the biggest problems for students; they are afraid to sell themselves. If you've got an impressive background, it won't help you to hide it or to avoid drawing special attention to it. If you believe that the admissions people will recognize your modesty and reward you, you're wrong. Either they will simply overlook your achievements or they will criticize you for not recognizing the strength of your own talents. The way to gain respect for your achievements is to highlight them. Not only does this highlighting show that you are proud of your work, but it will distinguish you from other applicants.

9. *Forgetting to photocopy the completed application and not having it sent by certified mail.*

Spend ten hours creating a one-thousand-word essay. Run around for three months collecting letters of recommendation. Sit in one place for an entire afternoon to type each page of your application. Now, throw everything into the waste basket.

That's what you'll be doing if you fail to make a photocopy of all your work, or if you turn cheap at the post office. Taking these special precautions is important because envelopes can get lost or destroyed. By sending applications certified (with a return-receipt), you will know that they've been received by the right person. Keeping a photocopy of your work can save you from having to remember or re-create an entirely new application if the admissions officer calls to say that his dog ate your essay or that a secretary lost it.

10. *Applying to too few schools.*

If you're too sure of yourself or overly thrifty, you will inevitably make this mistake. Every year, there are students who believe that they are certain to get into the top three law schools—so naturally they only bother applying to those three. Then they happen to get rejected. How much can it hurt to swallow some of that pride and apply to three or four schools below your top-three limit? Since you'll have to wait an entire twelve months to apply again after being rejected, it's smarter to apply to eight or nine schools the first time around.

Strategy #11

From the Inside: The Admissions Officer's Perspective

Students applying to law school generally do not get the opportunity to speak with an admissions officer, so we've done it for you. Here are excerpts from interviews with admissions officers from four different law schools. The ones selected represent a cross-section of the various types of schools: Harvard Law School, University of California at Los Angeles (UCLA) Law School, Northwestern Law School, and University of Connecticut Law School.

How important is an applicant's creativity when you evaluate a student's application and essay?

Northwestern: An essay that uses a great deal of creativity can help becauses it catches our attention and makes us look more closely, but by no means can creative talent disguise the facts in a student's application. If a student has a weak record, we will see it eventually.

UCLA: We know that all applicants aren't great writers, so a lack of creativity would not be held against you at UCLA. But the more talent you display in this area, the better.

Harvard: We give a general essay assignment because we want to put the burden of deciding what to write on the applicant. Don't think that you have to write like a law student. Write what you're comfortable with.

Univ. of Conn.: The word "creativity" is dangerous. Originality is what's important. Students should use the essay to show their uniqueness. We've seen some terribly personal essays written in the third person by students who feel they must use legal jargon and sound like young lawyers. This just isn't true.

Many students believe that the professors and other people they use as references will only write positive *letters of recommendation for them. Do you ever receive "recommendations" that are blatantly negative?*

Harvard: Yes, I have received some blatantly negative letters from references.

Northwestern: Some of them have been nonevaluative letters, which serve absolutely no advantage for the student, but I don't recall any blatantly negative letters.

Univ. of Conn.: Sometimes we receive blatantly negative letters. But generally the reference has already warned the student that he cannot write a positive one. Unfortunately, some students insist that the person write anyway, assuming the reference will be less harsh on paper.

UCLA: It's not common to receive blatantly negative letters, but some writers will imply that a student has left a mediocre impression. Students should ask writers who are enthusiastic about their application.

Can a letter of recommendation ever push a student over the line toward acceptance or rejection? Are they ever taken that seriously?

Univ. of Conn.: Not generally, but I recall one case where it did. We later learned that the negative letter was quite inaccurate. Rarely will these have a sole, damning effect though.

Northwestern: While a letter will never be the sole reason to reject or accept, a well-detailed letter will cause us to look more closely at the applicant.

Harvard: There can be an occasion when a recommendation letter is the most important factor in a student's application, and in our decision to reject or accept.

There are many myths about taking the LSAT more than once. When a student takes it and receives a low score, then takes it a second time and receives a higher score, which score do you use when deciding whether or not to admit the student?

UCLA: When a student takes the test more than once, we average the scores and use that number in the evaluation.

Northwestern: We always take the highest score. We never average a student's scores.

Univ. of Conn.: When the scores are close together, we usually average them. But if they are spread out, our tendency is to take the higher score because we realize that sometimes there are bad test situations. My advice to students is that they should only plan on taking the test one time.

Since there are many people who take time off to work before applying to law school, do you care about the type of employment experience they have?

Harvard: We definitely care about an applicant's work experience. Different experiences demonstrate different talents. And by the way, many of our accepted students have been out of college for quite a while when they apply. Last year, we accepted a class of students which ranged in age from seventeen to forty-nine years old.

Northwestern: An applicant's actual job is not as important as the letter that the employer may write for the applicant. Many of our applicants have worked in para-legal positions after college.

Univ. of Conn.: In past years, it mattered to us what type of employment an applicant was involved in, but it matters less now. Many recent college graduates have taken any jobs they could find. We have accepted applicants who were working as waiters or waitresses. Of course, if the applicant has been working for the past ten years, we would be especially interested in his or her work experiences and growth on the job.

Some students believe that law schools will always accept applicants who have perfect grades and scores. Would you ever turn down a student who has a top grade point average and a perfect LSAT score?

Univ. of Conn.: While it rarely happens, there are certainly situations where we would turn down an applicant with such an impressive transcript. If an applicant has a criminal record or other disturbing qualities, we must take them into account.

Harvard: We have turned down applicants who had an A-plus average and perfect LSAT scores, but it certainly doesn't occur that often.

Northwestern: I can't recall rejecting an applicant with perfect grades and scores.

UCLA: Because of our methods of admission, this can certainly happen. We admit 60% of our students by principal consideration on their grades and scores. The remaining 40% of the applicants are chosen more on the basis of their diversity and less on the basis of their transcripts. When examining an application, we ask ourselves, "Can we accept this person?" And that's much different from asking ourselves, "Can we reject them?" We try to fit the applicant into a group that can be accepted.

As admissions officers, is there anything else that you think applicants should know as they begin the law school application process?

Northwestern: Students should realize that any interview they receive with us will be for informational purposes only. Many of them believe incorrectly that interviews are used in the evaluation process, but they definitely are not.

UCLA: Don't think that an overly creative application can get you in—facts will get you into law school. If you're concerned about a low exam score or other special problem, put a note to that effect in your application. Be direct with the facts and appropriate explanations.

Harvard: Admissions committees differ from school to school. Our committee consists solely of faculty, but other schools include law students among the members.

Univ. of Conn.: Never be modest when filling out your application. What you don't tell us, we won't know. We don't have any methods for researching your unique achievements, so include everything that you feel is important.

Strategy #12

After Getting Accepted or Rejected

You might wonder why there is a chapter on what to do about rejections and acceptances. You either got in or you didn't, right? Well, not exactly. Law school admission is not always as cut and dried as college admission.

To begin with, there is no common date on which students are notified. There is no April 15 date when every pre-law student in the country dashes to the mailbox in search of the thick or thin envelope. As a matter of fact, students may be accepted or rejected anytime from the day the application is received at the office to the day before the law school actually opens its doors in September.

Acceptances

Most law schools will tell you if they have rolling admission. If you have applied to one that does, this means that your application will be considered as soon as it arrives at the office and that you'll receive an answer in a specified period of time following that day (usually four to five weeks). Under this system, a student with a strong record could be notified of his or her acceptance as early as December 1.

Most students don't hear whether they've been accepted until late March or early April, and a few schools will stick to their fixed notification dates of mid or late April. In either case, students generally have until the beginning or the middle of May to select a school and send in a deposit (usually around $250) to save a space.

Waiting List

Then there's that nerve-wracking waiting list. This is a limbo somewhere between getting accepted and being rejected. Many law schools will admit a certain number of students, then place a smaller number of students on the waiting list as alternates, because they are good candidates, but not as strong as those who were accepted. Once some of the accepted students decide *not* to attend the law school, the students on the waiting list are given a place in the class.

Unfortunately, you rarely have an idea of where on the list you've been placed. If you are second or third on the list, you probably have nothing to worry about, but if you're number forty-nine, you may not get in at all. Most schools never let you know where you stand, so the only thing you can do is send in more information or strong new recommendations that may improve your chances of joining the ranks of those accepted.

Rejections

Like acceptances, rejection letters may be mailed to students very early in the selection process. If you are a definite "no" candidate, the admissions people won't hesitate to forward a rejection to you via return mail. And in a way, it's good to know where you stand with each of the schools as early as possible.

Now it's important to talk about the possibilities of rejection. You must remember that no matter how many law schools reject your application, you should not take the letters personally. This can be an emotionally charged time in your life, but keep in mind that the law school is turning down your professional qualifications—not you as a person. And on top of the grades and scores, each law school may interpret your activities, your courses, your recommendations, your summer jobs, and your essay differently. While you may feel that you had more going for you than someone you know who got accepted, every case is viewed differently.

If you prefer to keep your rejection a secret from others, then don't tell *anyone*—bad news will always spread fast. Sometimes the most painful part of rejection is thinking that other people will lose respect for you. As horrible as it sounds, there will be students who take great satisfaction in knowing that you were rejected. Law-school competition can bring out the worst in people, so it may be better to just share your feelings with your family or your very close friends who are not attending your school.

The absolute worst thing you can do after being rejected is to get on the telephone and call the law-school admissions office. Many students think that they can pin the law school down and find out why they were not accepted. Even if you know that one of the students they accepted had a weaker record, it will do you absolutely no good. The best way to deal with this concern is to speak with your pre-law adviser and have him make the investigation.

Reapplying After Rejection

You may have noticed that many applications have a question that asks if you have ever applied to or been rejected by their school before. Though admissions people can offer a million reasons why they need to ask this question, you can be 99 percent sure that saying that you'd once been rejected is not going to help your chances this second time around.

But there are two reasons why you might reapply to a school after having been rejected. One is that you now have a more impressive record (maybe you've taken the LSAT again and raised your score). The second reason is that you believe that the admissions people rejected you by mistake (it *can* happen, but it's not common).

Improving Your Record After Being Wait-Listed

If there is any time to try to add to your record, it is once you've been placed on a school's waiting list. It is a do or die period during which you must try to raise your LSAT score, improve your grade point average, win a new award, become the president of a new activity, or collect another impressive recommendation. You may never have another chance, so you should do whatever you can to make yourself look better than the other wait-listed candidates.

Deferrals

Very few law schools make use of this form of acceptance. Though it's a common practice of some business schools to accept a student and then tell him that he cannot begin classes for another two years, law schools do not make much use of this. Deferrals are mainly used by business schools because they want a student to work in the business world and gain more "real world" skills before taking part in the classroom experience. When the term *deferral* is used in relation to law school, it usually means that a student who has been accepted is now asking to take a year off before beginning classes.

Getting the Decision Reversed

Though it is extremely difficult to do and though it hardly ever happens, it *is* possible to get a rejection reversed at some schools. If you can prove that the law school was not given the proper information (namely, that they received an incorrect or incomplete transcript or a misrepresented letter of recommendation), then maybe your case can be reconsidered. The best way to handle a special problem is through your pre-law adviser. And if your adviser feels you have a good case, maybe you should follow it up. Mistakes can happen. If both you and your adviser believe that you should have been accepted by a particular school, perhaps some mistake in the forwarding of records or scores was made.

The only other way you can get a decision reversed (and this method can be used in only a few schools) is if you happen to have important strings to pull. You will need, for instance, the assistance of wealthy alumni, relatives in the admissions office, and a few other connections that are best left unstated. It doesn't always work, but it may be worth trying.

Strategy #13

How to Pay for Law School

While there are some state law schools that charge in the area of $2,000 a year for tuition, there are many law schools which charge more than $6,000 each year. And on top of that, you can add the charges for housing, board, books, and other expenses. Parents and students often find themselves paying out as much as $16,000 each year for some of the more expensive law schools.

And, whether you plan on earning a lot of money one day or not, most students need some sort of financial aid when they begin law school. Although some of the forms have different names and many of the procedures have changed, law schools offer loans, grants, scholarships, and work-study programs, just as college did.

Loan Programs

You should be warned that the various provisions in government loan programs are always being altered. Because administrations and availability of funds change, you should be sure to speak to the financial aid office in your college or at the law school.

One of the most popular loan programs that exists today is the Guaranteed Student Loan (GSL). You may have heard of this under the name Federally Insured Student Loan (FISL) or the Higher Education Loan Program (HELP). One almost wonders why there would be so many names for the same thing. Is it because the federal government wants to confuse you? Not exactly. This loan is called "FISL" if the money is administered by the federal government and "GSL" if administered by a state agency. The most that you can borrow under the loans is $25,000.

What you must look into, though, is whether you have already borrowed under this program during college. If so, make sure you haven't used the entire $25,000. As of the publication of this book, these loans are available to any student whose yearly family income does not exceed $30,000 or to students whose family income exceeds $30,000 but who can show financial need (based on size of family, other family members in school, and so forth.) Under these loans, there are also provisions for students who have an independent status from their parents. In order to declare independent status, a student has to be living on his own for at least a year before application for the loan. There are other requirements that you can find out about by talking to the financial aid people at school.

Although the loans don't have to be paid back while you're still in law school, the interest rates can be set at either 7%, 8% or 9%, depending on when you began your first FISL or GSL loan. This loan can be repaid over a period of up to nine or ten years. In order to apply for these loans, you should speak to a loan officer at a bank in your area. The law schools have nothing to do with the granting of these loans.

National Direct Student Loans

Another loan program available to students is the National Direct Student Loan (NDSL), which many students take advantage of while in college. Although the provisions for this loan have changed in the past, the total loan you may receive from this program is $12,000. The interest rate is set at 5% and can be paid back over a period as long as ten years.

Federal "Plus" Loans

This third type of loan can provide law students with up to $3,000 each year, no matter how well-off your family is. While this seems exceedingly generous during a period of financial cutbacks, there is a catch. The "plus" loans are provided at commercial rates of interest. In addition, the lending bank can require you to begin repayment while you're still in school. Your parents are ultimately responsible for these loans.

State Loans

It is also a good idea to see what special loan programs your state has to offer. While most of the money comes from the federal government, some states have loans for students. Ask a local bank officer.

Before discussing the ways in which your law school can serve as lender, let's discuss a special form that you'll be hearing a lot about during your three years at law school.

The GAPSFAS Form

During college, most students hear about the Financial Aid Form (FAF)—that booklet full of green, white, and gray-shaded areas. Well, now that you're applying to law school, there is a new form. This financial statement is provided by the Graduate and Professional School Financial Aid Service (GAPSFAS) or the Educational Testing Service. The GAPSFAS form is a relatively simple yet visually confusing four-page questionnaire. Although it provides specific directions on how to answer the various financial questions, many students are discouraged from applying to schools for financial aid because it may take a great deal of time to fill it out properly.

You will need to complete this form if you want your school to consider awarding you any form of financial aid. For the GAPSFAS form, you will need your parents' income tax form as well as your own.

Borrowing from the Law School

If you have applied for a loan at a bank and have been refused, your law school can act as a lender. It will require you to submit a GAPSFAS form and perhaps other information if you want it to obtain the loans for you. The law school financial aid office can provide you with more information. Instead of repaying the government program directly, you may have to pay the school itself.

Special Grants and Scholarships

Although it has become much more difficult to find financial help that does not have to be paid back, students can still find grants and scholarships that are awarded by private institutions. Many corporations, foundations, and private endowments have small scholarships that students can compete for through essay writing or test taking. There are even special grants for students who happen to be residents of certain counties or cities.

The best way to learn about these additional resources is to ask each law school to send you brochures on special scholarships. They aren't likely to send this information to people who are too shy to ask for it.

Work-Study Programs

Another method by which students can help pay for law school is through a work-study plan determined by your school's financial aid office. Because there are always many jobs available on campus (in the library, dining hall, departmental offices, and elsewhere), many schools will help you pay your tuition by providing you with some sort of job. Because law school requires a great amount of time for class preparation, most work-study programs allow students to work in a paying job for no more than ten to fifteen hours each week.

In addition to figuring the money earned from the above program into your financial aid package, the law school will assume that you will be earning money over the summers. Each student is expected to contribute a certain amount of money from these summer earnings each year.

Scholarship Search Services

In the past few years, there have been several companies that have helped students who are in need of financial aid. The scholarship search companies utilize computers to research special scholarships for different students. By taking specific information about the student (ethnic background, religion, sex, special interests) and entering it into the computer, the search service can locate scholarship programs that are looking for students with a similar background. The service will then give the student a list of addresses that he can write to in order to apply for the specific scholarship programs. Most large cities have companies like this that charge a reasonable fee for the service.

If you need financial aid in order to pay for law school, don't hesitate to use it. Many middle-class people take advantage of it, so don't let pride stand in your way. Start researching loans and other resources as soon as possible.

Strategy #14

Surviving the First Year of Law School

Is it boring? Will the professors try to embarrass me? How much do I have to know before I get there? Do many people flunk out in the first year? Is there any truth to that *Paper Chase* story?

These are just a few questions that students ask as they prepare for law school. No matter how many encouraging words you hear from the pre-law adviser or the law school catalog, there are still going to be more questions. For many of us, the only way to learn what the experience is like is to live it ourselves or to speak with a student who's already there. For this reason, we will open this chapter with some remarks from a first-year law student.

A Conversation with a First-Year Law Student

David is now in his first year at Harvard Law School, a school that has earned a reputation for being one of the most challenging institutions in the world. Since we can't possibly speak about every law school, it will probably be most helpful to speak about one that has an outstanding reputation.

Q. Through movies and books like The Paper Chase *and* One L, *students have been given the impression that the whole law-school experience is like a living hell. Is it true?*

A. No. Most people are scared at the beginning because they don't want to be embarrassed, but it's a game that you shouldn't take too seriously.

Q. Is there a lot of homework in the first year?
A. Most students have two classes each day, and they spend about two hours each night to prepare for each class. You can spend from four to five hours each night throughout the year.

Q. Do you have assignments every day, or can you put them off until the weekend?
A. There's something every day. And you're expected to complete the assignment that night because the professor can call on you the next day to discuss the reading.

Q. Does the Socratic method embarrass people in class? Can you avoid being called on?
A. In first-year classes, most professors will use a seating chart, and will call out a name at random. It's embarrassing at first because no one wants to make a mistake, but you learn from the method. The only way to avoid answering is to say "pass," and after a while, *that* gets to be embarrassing. Most professors are trying to help you when they call your name. It forces you to get involved and learn the law.

Q. How can shy people handle the problem of speaking out in a group?
A. My advice is to say as little as possible in the beginning. The people who earned the worst reputations were the big mouths who tried to answer every question during the first weeks. Anyone who is applying to law school should realize that when first-year students arrive here, they know nothing about the law. So no one is at an advantage.

Q. What are the professors like?
A. They are brilliant, and they really want to teach you. While some are egomaniacs, they're all fair and very serious. Realize that many law professors have left high-paying jobs in law firms so that they could teach. They are here by *choice*—unlike some college professors.

Q. You spoke about fairness. How much does class participation count in the final grade for these classes that use the

Socratic method? Don't professors—even the fair ones—favor students who participate?

A. Participation has nothing to do with the final grade. Exam scores are used for your grades. Class participation is only important because it is their method of teaching you the law. And as far as grading is concerned, when professors score your exam, your name isn't on it. They only see your ID number—so being a favorite won't help you.

Q. Are the exams much different from those in college?

A. Students will find that it's no longer enough to just repeat everything that they heard in class. Law school exams are much less theoretical than the material that was discussed in that particular class. You really have to think analytically when taking the exams.

Q. Are there any shortcuts that students use in order to learn material faster or to study more effectively?

A. Some students use outlines, commercial summaries, and study guides. There are also academic summaries called "Horn books," but don't buy any of these things until you actually begin classes.

Q. For the students who dislike law school, what are their major complaints?

A. They say it's boring or time consuming, or too corporate. Some don't like the professors because many of them like to argue a lot. I think some people don't like it because they've got school work every night. And on top of that, no one is going to baby you along in law school.

Q. What about activities and social life? Is there any time for either?

A. Most students don't get very involved in activities until the second semester, but everyone has time for social life. There are many students who have time to hold an on-campus job. But whatever people do in their spare time, it usually relates to law in some way.

Q. Is it easy to find a summer job as a first-year law student?

A. If you start writing to firms early, you can get interviews, but most of the job hunt is done without the law school's aid.

The school mainly helps second- and third-year students find jobs. I had received summer job offers as early as November, just two months after school began. (David received high-paying offers long before the law firms even saw his first-semester grades.)

Words from Other First-Year Law Students

"I love it. The students here are brilliant, and you can learn so much from them." This was said by a first-year student at the University of Chicago Law School. "Everyone is into the topic. Though I'm glad I came here, I must admit that I haven't gone to the movies in a very long time."

A first-year student from Berkeley said that you don't have to study all the time in order to do well. "I still have time to waste time. I even keep up with the night-time soap operas." A student at Vanderbilt Law School agrees. "There are people who study all the time and still don't do well. It all depends on your attitude and your ability to focus your attention when you need to. With some practice, you learn what's important and what isn't." A student who just finished his first semester at Northwestern Law School admits, "the most important time during the semester is the few weeks before exams. During that period, you really learn to use your time effectively."

Now that you've heard the opinions of some students who are experiencing the challenges of law school's first year, let's continue and see what other concerns will face you in the first year of law school.

The Courses

It is easy to generalize when speaking about first-year courses. In almost every law school, the first two semesters will include the following courses: Contracts, Torts, Property, Civil Procedure, Criminal Law, Constitutional Law, Legal Writing, and one or two electives. Some courses last an entire year, but most last for just one semester. Since the smaller seminars and electives take place in the second and third years, most of your classes in the first year will be very large.

As most people aren't familiar with the course titles, here is a quick review of what each of the first-year courses offer:

- *Contracts:* the study of what is enforceable and what is not; the protection that contracts give to involved parties
- *Torts:* the study of compensating an injured party for damages; occurrences may include injuries that are intentional as well as unintentional
- *Property:* the study of the various rights surrounding land and other property ownership
- *Civil Procedure:* the study of the various phases of litigation (pleadings, trial, jurisdiction of the courts)
- *Criminal Law:* the study of the way we enforce criminal justice; constitutional and procedural concerns
- *Constitutional Law:* the study of the powers of various branches of government; purpose of judicial system

Other courses like Legal Writing and Moot Court are required by the Bar Association. The first trains students to perform legal research and to write legal briefs. Moot Court is a special way of training students in how the courts decide on particular cases. Moot Court allows students to argue a case and then hear how it is judged once both sides have been presented. Legal Writing and Moot Court are generally pass/fail courses, so it may be wise to devote most of your time to the other classes where you receive letter grades.

Review Courses

Believe it or not, there are actually six-week review courses that will help you prepare for law school. These reviews will give you a brief sample of the discussed courses, and they will tell you how to take notes and study for exams. If you can afford it, and if you're not doing anything during the summer before law school, it might help to register for a short course. Almost no one takes them, but if it will relieve your anxiety, it might be worthwhile.

The Case Method

Most courses are taught with the aid of case books, which supplement your reading with actual historical court cases. This is a practical way to understand the law. You will see that the law is very theoretical, and it won't really make sense to you until you can see how it has affected actual situations. While it seems like a lot of extra work to read and then reread a new case every evening, you'll realize that it makes the study of law much easier and much more practical.

The Books

The most important thing that you should know about textbooks and case books is that they are all different. Just because your cousin gave you his constitutional law textbook from Duke Law doesn't mean you can use it at Boston University Law School. The books are expensive, but don't go shopping around for bargains until you've actually arrived on campus. Every professor has his or her own favorite text, and any text may be in the process of being revised. Make sure you've got the newest edition before shelling out all that money.

You should also note that you can purchase various law summaries. These publications are very popular because they make class preparation much simpler. The summaries only cost a few dollars and are available in editions that include everything from administrative law to contracts to trusts and wills. While professors realize that students use them, it's a good idea to keep them locked away in your room.

And according to one law student from Ohio, the most important book of all is *Black's Law Dictionary*. Every student should have his or her own copy from the day he begins classes.

Performing in Class

Assuming that you've done your homework before arriving in class, you should always be prepared to give the important facts of a case when you're called on. You should also be prepared to explain how and why the court ruled as it did. In other words, you should understand the reasoning behind its actions. All of this seems complicated, but it is actually the *least* that you should know when you enter the classroom each day.

Students should also be prepared to discuss the case by giving their own opinions on the rulings. If this means that you must shoot holes in the court's ruling, then do it. But at the same time, be prepared for the professor to set you up, as well as tear you down. Don't be afraid to put yourself in this situation, though. The more you say and the more questions you're asked, the more likely it is you will learn the material. This is not the time or place to be shy.

Study Groups

You've probably heard about the study groups that help most first year students through their courses. Usually consisting of four or five students in the same class, these groups are formed in order to study material more efficiently. Once you begin your classes at the beginning of each semester, it's a good idea to look around the classroom and consider organizing a study group with a few of the more reliable students.

Some students form groups with their roommates or their friends, but it's best to avoid anyone who is too chummy. You're likely to turn the session into a social gathering if you enjoy each other's company too much. Each person should be assigned to outline a certain course or a certain number of assignments from each course. Through semiweekly or weekly meetings, your study group can work to review, pose interesting questions, and prepare for exams long before they arrive.

One University of Chicago law student suggests that you not hesitate to kick out any study group member who fails to contribute. "We kicked a guy out of our group because he was just *too* smart. Since he learned the material very easily, he spent little time studying and only contributed sloppy outlines to the group." It can be just as troublesome when you study with a person who is too slow to understand the material, so choose your group carefully.

Preparing for the Exams

You'll be glad to know that there are no surprise quizzes or midterm tests in law school. But what you won't be so glad about is the fact that almost all of your grades will be riding on one exam. Since these final exams determine your grades in law school, you can't take them lightly. You can forget about cramming on the night before because there's just too much to read and remember.

Two graduates who managed to maintain an A average in their first year at a west-coast law school agreed on the following suggestions for studying for final exams:

- Begin studying for your exams at least two or three weeks in advance.
- Collect all the summaries and outlines that you can get.
- Study everything on your own, at least twice.
- Organize a study group of four or fewer people, and meet with them only after you understand the material.
- Speak to second-year law students and ask them to recall your course, your professor, and the final exam.
- Draw up outlines to study from—and keep them brief.
- Be prepared for exam questions that will try to affect you emotionally. Learn to look only at the facts of a case.
- If you can see copies of old exams (legally, of course) then do so.
- Don't study with classmates who are the red-hot, nervous types. They will only destroy your confidence.

Strategy #15

Eight Myths (and Eight Facts) About the Legal Profession

Just as there are popular myths about the law school admissions process, there are myths about the actual practice of law. Instead of being deluded by these stories for the next three years, you should know what it's really going to be like in the real world. You will see that things are quite different from what you've heard, and that the entire profession offers many exciting challenges.

MYTH #1: *The best route to follow when leaving law school is to begin in a small suburban or rural law firm, and then work your way up to the larger ("factory size") firms in major cities.*

FACT: Many students believe that the legal profession is similar to others where one is supposed to start small and then later shoot for the big pie in the sky. If you have a dream of one day working for some major Chicago or Dallas law firm, the last thing you want to do is spend the first five years of your legal career in a small, nondescript firm. The benefit of entering a large firm right after law school is that you receive training in many areas. The large firms have certain departments and partners who specialize in entertainment law, tax law, litigation, and other fields. It's better to learn everything in the big firms, and *then* move (if you want) to a smaller firm where you can show off your many talents.

MYTH #2: *There is basically no way to tie in your own special interests with the practice of law.*

FACT: If you have a particular hobby or educational degree that you would like to tie in with your future law practice, there is almost always some way to do it. If you're a movie industry buff, maybe you should consider entertainment law. With a college background in foreign affairs, you may want to enter international law. There's environmental law for those who are interested in conservation, or tax law if you've got a background in finance. There are an infinite number of combinations. Although it might take a few years after law school before you are able to zero in on your own special interests, you can certainly do it.

MYTH #3: *If you don't want to live in Chicago, New York City, Washington, D.C., or Los Angeles, then law is not for you.*

FACT: Although it's true that each of these cities has a high concentration of law firms, by no means will you find that every successful lawyer has to be based in these places. Lawyers are needed wherever there are people or businesses. Not only are there many suburban areas in need of lawyers, but there are many less developed areas where "country lawyers" join or establish very successful practices.

MYTH #4: *Corporate law is the only area of law that will ensure your financial success.*

FACT: There are really two myths hidden behind this statement. The first is that corporate law will ensure your financial success. While it's true that some corporate law firms pay terrific starting salaries, there is absolutely no area of law that can guarantee your financial success. Besides the common-sense issues of managing your money and living within your means, you can lose your job at any point, in any type of law. Corporate firms can merge and cut the salaries, or let go of associates just like those firms that practice criminal law, or legal groups which are affiliated with the government or with nonprofit organizations.

The second aspect of this myth is that the only legal

positions which pay well are those that are affiliated with the corporate sector. This is not true. While everyone may not reach the same salary levels, a lawyer can become extremely successful in areas as unlikely as divorce or personal injury law. Marvin Mitchelson and Melvin Belli are just two attorneys who entered nontraditional practices of law and then turned them into gold mines.

MYTH #5: *It takes at least five or six years to become a partner in a good law firm.*

FACT: Good luck! Unlike many accounting firms, most of the quality law firms will wait at least eight or nine years before offering partnership to one of their associates. And you should know that each of those eight or nine years will consist of extended working hours and often monotonous duties that are performed simply in support of senior partners.

MYTH #6: *Once you enter the corporate law field, you can forget about ever performing not-for-profit legal work.*

FACT: All respectable corporate law firms perform a small amount of *pro bono* work—services for the public good. Whether those firms are volunteering in order to pacify their own guilty consciences for paying their young associates a thousand dollars a week or because they honestly believe in helping the underprivileged, there are many groups and individuals who benefit from these services.

MYTH #7: *The best way to identify the right law firm for you is by the high salary that it pays its first year associates.*

FACT: It's very difficult to invest $30,000 into your college education, add $35,000 more for three years at law school, and then turn down a $40,000 offer made to you by a well-respected law firm. While some students select a job at a particular firm solely on the basis of its starting salary, this can be a foolish move. There are so many other things to consider when choosing the right law firm—the areas of specialization, the size, the personalities of the partners and other associates. What's right for someone else may not be right for you.

MYTH #8: *What you study in law school is similar to the work you will be performing as a young lawyer.*

FACT: There is absolutely no law school that will train you to perform the practical duties of a lawyer. No matter how much practical (or clinical) experience a law school claims to give you, it only exists to teach you theory. Occasionally, you will find the opportunity to take a course on legal methods or legal research, but even this will not tell you how to treat your clients or how to deal with fellow associates and demanding partners. Your summer jobs and your conversations with practicing attorneys are the only true methods for learning about what a lawyer really does on the job.

Strategy #16

Finishing Up: Advice from a Third-Year Law Student

In order to give you an honest account of what happens after that often-devastating first-year experience, this chapter is primarily devoted to a conversation with a third-year student from a top law school. Since Art is currently making the transition from law school to the real world, he is able to look back on three years of law-school experience as well as describe the concerns of job hunting, the bar exam, and future career choices.

Q. Which was the most difficult year of law school?
A. The first year, by far. That's when you feel the pressure of getting good grades and of going to every single class.

Q. Do most second- and third-year students have a light work load?
A. It's not that it's a light work load. It's just that they *choose* not to work as hard. Third-year students usually have job offers by the fall months, so grades don't matter so much to them after that. Although some people keep a steady pace, many third-year students often don't even attend class. Some don't even bother to buy the books during that last year.

Q. Can it be assumed, then, that there is time for extracurricular activities once you've gotten past the second year?
A. Definitely. Not only do most students have part-time jobs, but I know some classmates who work at paying jobs for thirty-five to forty hours each week. I'm an editor on the law journal, and I also play on a squash team.

Q. Are there any other activities available?

A. There's always the school newspaper, moot court, other journals or reviews.

Q. Law Review is always a popular topic with pre-law students. Tell us something about it.

A. Each law school has a review or primary journal that is published a few times each year. These two- or three-hundred page paperbacks consist of legal articles and notes on cases or issues of interest to the legal scholar or practitioner. While these reviews are not written in an entertaining style, they are always well researched and extremely helpful when working on your own projects.

The primary articles in a law review are written by important professors or lawyers who have a special interest in a particular area of the law—they don't have to have any connection to your law school. The editorial staff of the law review is made up of students from your school who might do additional research on the articles or add to the notes at the end of each issue.

The reason it's so prestigious to be invited onto the law review is that it requires a great deal of time and intelligence. Most law schools will invite first-year students who have maintained an A average in their classes. Almost every law school also utilizes the writing competition method as a way to select new members of the law review. Rarely will a person turn down the opportunity to join law review—it's a good thing for resume.

Q. Have you found a job yet?

A. Yes, I had several job offers by the early part of the fall. I'll be working for a major Park Avenue law firm in New York. (Art's starting salary is large enough to buy one of the more expensive Mercedes-Benz cars.)

Q. Describe your job-hunting experiences.

A. Well, my first law office job was during the summer after the first year—and I spent that in an attorney general's office. During the second year of law school, I interviewed with law firms on campus. Like most law schools, mine is especially helpful to second- and third-year law students. I accepted a summer job at a corporate law firm which paid very well. Although some students choose to return to their old second-year jobs after graduation, I decided to interview elsewhere for my first full-time position.

Q. What are the job interviews like?

A. There is a lot of wining and dining. Although the firms are often very conservative, the interviews will often become social. There does not seem to be much emphasis on grades if you attended a good school. And if you're on Law Review, they almost don't care what your grade point average is. When you interview on campus, there is usually just one person in the room. The interviewer spends twenty minutes with each student talking about your courses, your interests, and your experience. By the way, my school asks students not to put their grades on their resumes. It cuts down on the competition.

Q. When you interviewed for full-time jobs, was it any different?

A. It's basically the same, but with full-time jobs, there are more call-backs. A call-back occurs if the interviewer liked you at the first meeting. You will then be asked to visit the law firm and spend a half day with them. You get to talk to five or six attorneys, and then they take you out for an expensive lunch or dinner. I have a friend who received call-backs from firms in New York, Los Angeles, Texas, and Atlanta. He was flying all over the country, staying in hotels and dining at the best restaurants—all at the expense of the law firms, of course.

Q. Do you have any advice for students who will be interviewing for jobs?

A. Yes, read *The American Lawyer*. This magazine has an annual survey of the country's major law firms. Also, don't be blinded by the salary offers. Spend the time to meet with as many attorneys at each firm as possible. I visited one firm three times in order to see if I liked it.

Q. Once you get a job offer, how much time do you have to decide to accept it or turn it down?

A. Usually one or two months.

Q. What information has the career placement office given to you?

A. We can get counseling on career opportunities, as well as specific information on applying for jobs. Although they don't train us to prepare for the bar exam, the placement office is a valuable help in planning one's future.

Q. Tell us about the bar exam.

A. Every state gives its own bar exam, so everyone studies different material. It is usually a two-day exam, and may be given twice a year in each state. Like most people, I'll be taking a study course during the summer. Since I already know where I'm working next year, I'll take the exam in late July and then go to Europe. My job starts in October and they've promised me a bonus so I can get reimbursed for the bar review course.

Final Words

For those of you who have been worried by law-school horror stories, it should now be clear that there are many rewards awaiting the law school graduate. Yes, it's true that it's difficult to get in. But once you're in, and once you've survived the demands of the first year, you'll appreciate all that you've learned—and even more than that, you'll appreciate the career that you've just begun.

Strategy #17

The Get-into-Law-School Calendar

Don't wait until the last minute to prepare for law-school admissions. You can get into the law school of your choice by making all the right moves while you're in college. Starting as early as freshman year or as late as senior year (but *don't* wait until then), the "Get-into-Law-School Calendar" will lead you month by month through college and tell you what to do when.

There are special exams and study courses to take, applications to prepare and letters to mail. Don't memorize all of these things—rely on this calendar.

Freshman Year

September–October
Arrange a meeting with your new academic adviser and make a tentative schedule of college courses for the next two years. Explore the clubs, sports, and other extracurricular activities available. Drop in at the career placement office and pick up some law-school catalogs. Save them for future reading.

November–December
Now that you're settled into your classes, develop a good rapport with your professors by contributing to class discussion. Remember, you'll later be coming to them for recommendations. If you think you'll need help for finals, organize a study group or find a tutor.

January–February
If you haven't done so already, stop by the dean or president's

office and introduce yourself. Even if you just want to tell them that you like your courses, they will appreciate and remember your comments.

March–April
Meet with your adviser or dean again and plan your courses for next year. Keep your college's requirements in mind. Start making plans for your summer months (summer school, job, travel).

May–June
Approach your favorite professors from this year and ask them for letters of recommendation. Put them on file in the departmental or dean's offices. Ease up on extracurricular activities and prepare for finals.

July–August
Use the summer to read through some of those law school applications and see what types of questions they ask. Before ending your summer job, ask your employer for a written recommendation. Send a thank-you note to the employer—this may help you get the job again next summer.

Sophomore Year

September–October
Start new courses and make good first impressions on professors. Continue last year's activities or join others, but try concentrating on just a couple. Aim for a leadership position in one of your activities.

November–December
Read some of the law-school catalogs and meet with the pre-law adviser to discuss your interest in law school. Think of signing up for one of the college courses that provides good legal skills (Introductory Logic, Constitutional Interpretation, etc.). Use the holiday season as a time to talk to recent college grads who are now in law school.

January–February
Stop by and chat with a few of the administrators. You may

want to visit the alumni office and get addresses of practicing attorneys who are willing to meet with you and give you ideas on your future legal career.

March–April
Start looking for a challenging summer job. Perhaps working in a law office or law library will be good for your record. Work hard in your activities so that you can get a leadership position by next year. Find out if your school has a pre-law society, and take advantage of their programs.

May–June
Try to do well on your finals and get letters of recommendation from professors who gave you the highest grades. Talk to some seniors who have been accepted by law schools and find out what the application process was like for them.

July–August
Buy an LSAT review book and spend a few hours reviewing a sample test. If you're working in a law office, try to meet some of the attorneys. Maybe they can give you advice or later write a recommendation.

Junior Year

September
Send away to three or four law schools for catalogs and applications. Even though these are not the applications that you'll use, they're good to look over. Find out if by next year, you'll have enough information to fill in the blanks. Ask the pre-law adviser about scholarships and graduate school loans.

October
Try to gain leadership positions in your activities. Work hard in your courses. Your junior-year grades will probably be the last ones on your transcript by the time you apply to the law schools.

November
Review some exams in your LSAT study book. Ask the pre-law adviser for one or two past exams. Many colleges keep them on file in the career placement office.

December
Find out about LSAT review courses. If you're taking the test in late spring, you may want to register for the review course now or during the next few weeks. Read through as many law-school catalogs as possible and consider their size, distance, cost, level of competition, etc.

January
Meet with your pre-law adviser and have him or her suggest some possible law schools, based on your grades. Look into a summer pre-law program.

February
Continue to study for the LSAT. If your college invites law-school admissions people to campus for informational meetings, attend them and ask questions.

March
If you want to take the late spring LSAT, it may be about time to register for it. Think about next year's courses and try to select ones that will look especially challenging to the admissions people. Also make sure you've fulfilled your own college's requirements.

April
Try to get as prestigious a summer job as possible. Though it doesn't have to be law related, it should be something that will look good on your application.

May
Do as well as possible on final exams. Visit this semester's professors and any deans you know, and ask them for letters of recommendation. Since most students will wait until September to do this, they'll have time to write yours now. Meet with your pre-law adviser and discuss your favorite law schools. Have your adviser look at the past records of students who got into those schools.

June
Even if you don't know the exact law schools to which you'll be applying, send away for the new applications. They're all free, so get as many as you can.

July
If you have any free time this summer, you may want to visit a few of the law schools that interest you. Call in advance and arrange to take a tour of the campus. Try to sit in on some of the first-year classes too.

August
Those of you who didn't take the late spring LSAT should register for the one given during the fall. You may want to take an LSAT review course if you can't keep to your own study schedule.

Senior Year

September
Organize your applications, catalogs, and financial aid forms in a neat file and begin working on the ones that are due earliest. Make sure that you have a good selection of recommendation letters. Be certain that you understand how the LSDAS system works. It can be confusing as you begin the application process.

October
Meet with your pre-law adviser and narrow down your list of law schools. Continue to research scholarships and other financial aid resources if you feel you'll need them. When the law school admissions people visit your campus, go to the sessions and meet them. Make an impression—sometimes they'll remember you.

November
If you took the fall LSAT, you should have your scores by the end of this month. Make a realistic judgment of your chances for admission to certain schools. Complete all of the forms that ensure that your college transcript and LSAT scores are sent to the right places.

December
This month is probably the last time that you can take the LSAT if you want to attend law school next year, so register as soon as possible. Try to complete all of your applications by the

middle of December. The flood of applications occurs during the holidays, so try to get yours in earlier.

January
If you know any law-school alumni or have high-powered contacts, ask them to help you. Since it's now or never, being shy will get you nowhere. Now that your applications are all in, you may want to contact each school and politely ask if your file is missing anything (letters of recommendation, transcript, LSAT scores, etc.).

February–March
Continue to look for scholarships and other sources of financial aid. Send law schools any supplementary material like new awards, or anything else that may help your candidacy. Keep your grades up just in case law schools make a spot check. It's not common, but it can happen.

April
Keep your fingers crossed! You'll probably hear the ruling some time this month. Once you've heard from your schools, it may help your final decision if you visit the campuses one last time or look at the law school's placement records.

Appendix

Law Schools Approved by the American Bar Association

The following is a list of the law schools that are recognized by the American Bar Association. In addition to giving phone numbers and addresses where you can write for more information, the list will tell you whether the institution is private or public. The list of 172 schools is given alphabetically by state.

Alabama

Samford University
Cumberland School of Law
800 Lakeshore Drive
Birmingham 35229
(205) 870-2701
(private)

University of Alabama
School of Law
P.O. Box 1435
University 34586
(205) 348-5750
(public)

Arizona

Arizona State University
College of Law
Tempe 85287
(602) 965-6181
(public)

University of Arizona
College of Law
Tuscon 85721
(602) 626-1373
(public)

Arkansas

University of Arkansas
School of Law
Waterman Hall
Fayetteville 72701
(501) 575-5601
(public)

University of Arkansas at Little Rock
School of Law
400 West Markam
Little Rock 72201
(501) 371-1071
(public)

California

California Western School of Law
350 Cedar Street
San Diego 92101
(619) 239-0391
(private)

Golden Gate University
School of Law
536 Mission Street
San Francisco 94105
(415) 442-7250
(private)

Loyola Law School
1441 West Olympic Boulevard
Los Angeles 90015
(213) 736-1000
(private)

Pepperdine University
School of Law
Malibu 90265
(213) 456-4611
(private)

Southwestern University
School of Law
675 South Westmoreland Avenue
Los Angeles 90005
(213) 738-6700
(private)

Stanford Law School
Stanford 94305
(415) 497-2465
(private)

University of California
School of Law
Boalt Hall
Berkeley 94720
(415) 642-1741
(public)

University of California
School of Law
King Hall
Davis 95616
(916) 752-0243
(public)

University of California
School of Law
405 Hilgard Avenue
Los Angeles 90024
(213) 825-4841
(public)

University of California
Hastings College of the Law
200 McAllister Street
San Francisco 94102
(415) 557-0448
(public)

University of the Pacific
McGeorge School of Law
3200 Fifth Avenue
Sacramento 95817
(916) 739-7191
(private)

University of San Diego
School of Law
Acala Park
San Diego 92110
(714) 293-4527
(private)

University of San Francisco
School of Law
2130 Fulton Street
San Francisco 94117
(415) 666-6307
(private)

University of Santa Clara
School of Law
Santa Clara 95053
(408) 984-4361
(private)

University of Southern California
The Law Center
University Park
Los Angeles 90089-0071
(213) 743-6473
(private)

Whittier College
School of Law
5353 West Third Street
Los Angeles 90020
(213) 938-3621
(private)

Colorado

University of Colorado
School of Law
Campus Box 401
Boulder 80309
(303) 492-8047
(public)

University of Denver
College of Law
200 West 14th Avenue
Denver 80204
(303) 753-2645
(private)

Connecticut

University of Bridgeport
School of Law
303 University Avenue
Bridgeport 06601
(203) 576-4041
(private)

University of Connecticut
School of Law
West Hartford 06117
(203) 241-4633
(public)

Yale Law School
P.O. Box 401A Yale Station
New Haven 06520
(203) 436-8995
(private)

Delaware

Delaware Law School
Widener University
P.O. Box 7474
Wilmington 19803
(302) 478-3000
(private)

District of Columbia

American University
Washington College of Law
4400 Massachusetts Avenue, NW
Washington 20016
(202) 686-2605
(private)

Antioch School of Law
2633 16th Street, NW
Washington 20009
(202) 265-9500
(private)

Catholic University of America
School of Law
Washington, 20064
(202) 635-5144
(private)

Georgetown University Law Center
600 New Jersey Avenue, NW
Washington, 20001
(202) 624-8000
(private)

George Washington University
The National Law Center
720 20th Street, N.W.
Washington, 20052
(202) 676-6592
(private)

Howard University
School of Law
2900 Van Ness Street, N.W.
Washington, 20008
(202) 686-6837
(private)

Florida

Florida State University
College of Law
Tallahassee, 32306
(904) 644-3400
(public)

Nova University
Center for the Study of Law
3100 Southwest 9th Avenue
Fort Lauderdale, 33315
(305) 522-2300
(private)

Stetson University
College of Law
1401 61st Street South
St. Petersburg, 33707
(813) 345-1300
(private)

University of Florida
College of Law
Spessard L. Holland Law Center
Gainesville, 32611
(904) 392-0421
(public)

University of Miami
School of Law
P.O. Box 248087
Coral Gables, 33124
(305) 384-2392
(private)

Georgia

Emory University
School of Law
Atlanta 30322
(404) 329-6815
(private)

Mercer University
Walter F. George School of Law
Macon 31207
(912) 744-2601
(private)

University of Georgia
School of Law
Athens 30602
(404) 542-7140
(public)

Hawaii

University of Hawaii
School of Law
1400 Lower Campus
Honolulu 96822
(808) 948-7966
(public)

Idaho

University of Idaho
College of Law
Moscow 83843
(208) 885-6422
(public)

Illinois

DePaul University
College of Law
25 East Jackson Boulevard
Chicago 60604
(312) 321-7700
(private)

Illinois Institute of Technology
Chicago-Kent College of Law
77 South Wacker Drive
Chicago 60606
(312) 567-5000
(private)

The John Marshall Law School
315 South Plymouth Court
Chicago 60604
(312) 427-2737
(private)

Loyola University
School of Law
1 East Pearson Street
Chicago 60611
(312) 670-2920
(private)

Northern Illinois University
College of Law
DeKalb 60115
(815) 753-1067
(public)

Northwestern University
School of Law
357 East Chicago Avenue
Chicago 60615
(312) 649-8462
(private)

Southern Illinois University
School of Law
Carbondale 62901
(618) 536-7711
(public)

University of Chicago
Law School
1111 East 60th Street
Chicago 60637
(312) 753-2401
(private)

University of Illinois
College of Law
504 East Pennsylvania Avenue
Champaign 61820
(217) 333-0931
(public)

Indiana

Indiana University
School of Law
Bloomington 47405
(812) 335-8885
(public)

Indiana University
School of Law—Indianapolis
735 West New York Street
Indianapolis 46202
(317) 264-8523
(public)

University of Notre Dame
Law School
Notre Dame 46556
(219) 283-6627
(private)

Valparaiso University
School of Law
Valparaiso 46383
(219) 464-5346
(private)

Iowa

Drake University
Law School
Des Moines 50311
(515) 271-2824
(private)

University of Iowa
College of Law
Iowa City 52242
(319) 353-5742
(public)

Kansas

University of Kansas
School of Law
Lawrence 66045
(913) 864-4550
(public)

Washburn University of Topeka
School of Law
1700 College
Topeka 66621
(913) 295-6660
(private)

Kentucky

Northern Kentucky University
Salmon P. Chase College of Law
1401 Dixie Highway
Covington 41011
(606) 572-5340
(public)

University of Kentucky
College of Law
209 Law Building
Lexington 40506
(606) 257-1678
(public)

University of Louisville
School of Law
Belknap Campus
Louisville 40292
(502) 588-6358
(public)

Louisiana

Louisiana State University
The Paul M. Hebert Law Center
Baton Rouge 70813
(504) 388-8491
(public)

Loyola University
School of Law
6363 St. Charles Avenue
New Orleans 70118
(504) 865-2261
(private)

Southern University
School of Law
Southern Branch Post Office
Baton Rouge 70813
(504) 771-2552
(public)

Tulane University
School of Law
6801 Ferret Street
New Orleans 70118
(504) 865-5939
(private)

Maine

University of Maine
School of Law
246 Deering Avenue
Portland 04102
(207) 780-4340
(public)

Maryland

University of Baltimore
School of Law
1420 North Charles Street
Baltimore 21201
(301) 625-3170
(public)

University of Maryland
School of Law
500 West Baltimore Street
Baltimore 21201
(public)

Massachusetts

Boston College
Law School
885 Centre Street
Newton Centre 02159
(617) 969-0100
(private)

Boston University
School of Law
765 Commonwealth Avenue
Boston 02215
(617) 353-3112
(private)

Harvard Law School
Cambridge 02138
(617) 495-3100
(private)

New England School of Law
154 Stuart Street
Boston 02116
(617) 451-0010
(private)

Northeastern University
School of Law
400 Huntington Avenue
Boston 02115
(617) 437-4931
(private)

Suffolk University
Law School
41 Temple Street
Boston 02114
(617) 723-4700
(private)

Western New England College
School of Law
1215 Wilbraham Road
Springfield 01119
(413) 782-3111
(private)

Michigan

Detroit College of Law
130 East Elizabeth Street
Detroit 48201
(313) 965-0150
(private)

Thomas M. Cooley Law School
217 South Capitol Avenue
P.O. Box 13038
Lansing 48901
(517) 371-5140
(private)

University of Detroit
School of Law
651 East Jefferson Avenue
Detroit 48226
(313) 961-5444
(private)

University of Michigan
Law School
Hutchins Hall
Ann Arbor 48109
(313) 764-1358
(public)

Wayne State University
Law School
468 West Ferry
Detroit 48202
(313) 577-3930
(public)

Minnesota

Hamline University
School of Law
1536 Hewitt Avenue
St. Paul 55104
(612) 641-2400
(private)

University of Minnesota
Law School
285 Law Center
Minneapolis 55455
(617) 373-2717
(public)

William Mitchell College of Law
875 Summit Avenue
St. Paul 55105
(612) 227-9171
(private)

Mississippi

Mississippi College
School of Law
151 East Griffith Street
Jackson 39201
(601) 944-1950
(private)

University of Mississippi
School of Law
University 38677
(601) 233-7361
(public)

Missouri

St. Louis University
School of Law
3700 Lindell Boulevard
St. Louis 63208
(314) 658-2760
(private)

University of Missouri—Columbia
School of Law
Tate Hall
Columbia 65211
(314) 882-6487
(public)

University of Missouri—Kansas City
5100 Rockhill Road
Kansas City 64110
(816) 276-1644
(public)

Washington University
School of Law
Box 1120
St. Louis 63130
(314) 889-6400
(private)

Montana

University of Montana
School of Law
Missoula 59812
(406) 243-4311
(public)

Nebraska

Creighton University
School of Law
2500 California Street
Omaha 68178
(401) 280-2872
(private)

University of Nebraska
College of Law
Lincoln 68583-0902
(401) 472-2161
(public)

New Hampshire

Franklin Pierce Law Center
2 White Street
Concord 03301
(603) 228-1541
(private)

New Jersey

Rutgers—The State University of New Jersey
School of Law
Fifth and Penn Streets
Camden 08102
(609) 757-6398
(public)

Rutgers—The State University of New Jersey
School of Law
S.I. Newhouse Center for Law & Justice
15 Washington Street
Newark, 07102
(201) 648-5561
(public)

Seton Hall University
School of Law
111 Raymond Boulevard
Newark 07102
(201) 642-8500
(private)

New Mexico

University of New Mexico
School of Law
1117 Stanford, N.E.
Albuquerque 87131
(505) 277-2146
(public)

New York

Brooklyn Law School
250 Joralemon Street
Brooklyn 11201
(212) 625-2200
(private)

Columbia University
School of Law
435 West 116th Street
New York 10027
(212) 280-2675
(private)

Cornell Law School
Myron Taylor Hall
Ithaca 14853
(607) 256-3626
(private)

Fordham University
School of Law
140 West 62nd Street
New York 10023
(212) 841-5193
(private)

Hofstra University
School of Law
Hempstead 11550
(516) 560-6600
(private)

New York Law School
57 Worth Street
New York 10013
(212) 966-3500
(private)

New York University
School of Law
40 Washington Square South
New York 10012
(212) 598-2511
(private)

Pace University
School of Law
78 North Broadway
White Plains 10603
(914) 682-7200
(private)

St. John's University
School of Law
Fromkes Hall
Grand Central & Utopia Parkways
Jamaica 11439
(212) 990-6161
(private)

State University of New York
at Buffalo
John Lord O'Brian Hall
Amherst Campus
Buffalo 14260
(716) 636-2061
(public)

Syracuse University
College of Law
E.I. White Hall
Syracuse 13210
(315) 423-2524
(private)

Union University
Albany Law School
80 New Scotland Avenue
Albany 12208
(518) 445-2311
(private)

Yeshiva University
Benjamin N. Cardozo School of Law
55 Fifth Avenue
New York 10003
(212) 790-0463
(private)

North Carolina

Campbell University
School of Law
P.O. Box 158
Buies Creek 27506
(919) 893-4111
(private)

Duke University
School of Law
Durham 27706
(919) 684-2838
(private)

North Carolina Central University
School of Law
1801 Fayetteville Street
Durham 27707
(919) 683-6333
(public)

University of North Carolina
School of Law
Chapel Hill 27514
(919) 926-5106
(public)

Wake Forest University
School of Law
P.O. Box 7206
Reynolds Station
Winston-Salem 27109
(919) 761-5434
(private)

North Dakota

University of North Dakota
School of Law
Grand Forks 58202
(701) 777-2104
(public)

Ohio

Capital University
Law School
665 South High Street
Columbus 43215
(614) 445-8836
(private)

Case Western Reserve University
11075 East Boulevard
Cleveland 44106
(216) 368-3280
(private)

Cleveland State University
Cleveland-Marshall College of Law
Cleveland 44115
(216) 687-2344
(public)

Ohio Northern University
Claude W. Pettit College of Law
Ada 45810
(419) 634-9921
(private)

Ohio State University
College of Law
1659 North High Street
Columbus 43210
(614) 422-2631
(public)

The University of Akron
School of Law
302 East Buchtel Avenue
Akron 44325
(216) 375-7331
(public)

University of Cincinnati
College of Law
M.L. 40
Cincinnati 45221
(513) 475-6805
(public)

University of Dayton
School of Law
Dayton 45469
(513) 229-3211
(private)

University of Toledo
College of Law
2801 West Bancroft Street
Toledo 43606
(419) 537-2882
(public)

Oklahoma

Oklahoma City University
School of Law
2501 North Blackwelder
Oklahoma City 73106
(405) 521-5337
(private)

Oral Roberts University
O.W. Coburn School of Law
7777 South Lewis Avenue
Tulsa 74171
(918) 495-6039
(private)

University of Oklahoma
College of Law
300 Timberdell Road
Norman 73019
(405) 329-8800
(public)

University of Tulsa
College of Law
3120 East 4th Place
Tulsa 74104
(918) 592-6000
(private)

Oregon

Lewis and Clark College
Northwestern School of Law
10015 Southwest Terwilliger Blvd.
Portland 97219
(503) 244-1181
(private)

University of Oregon
School of Law
1101 Kincaid Street
Eugene 97403
(503) 686-3852
(public)

Willamette University
College of Law
250 Winter Street, S.E.
Salem 97301
(503) 370-6380
(private)

Pennsylvania

Dickinson School of Law
150 South College Street
Carlisle 17013
(717) 243-4611
(private)

Duquesne University
School of Law
900 Locust Street
Hanley Hall
Pittsburgh 15282
(412) 434-6300
(private)

Temple University
School of Law
1719 North Broad Street
Philadelphia 19122
(215) 787-7863
(public)

University of Pennsylvania
Law School
3400 Chestnut Street
Philadelphia 19104
(215) 243-7483
(private)

University of Pittsburgh
School of Law
3900 Forbes Avenue
Pittsburgh 15260
(412) 624-6200
(public)

Villanova University
School of Law
Villanova 19085
(215) 645-7000
(private)

Puerto Rico

Catholic University of Puerto Rico
School of Law
Ponce 00732
(809) 844-4150
(private)

Inter-American University of
Puerto Rico
School of Law
P.O. Box 8897
Fernandes Juncos Station
Santurce 00919
(809) 727-1930
(private)

University of Puerto Rico
School of Law
P.O. Box AZU P.R. Station
Rio Piedras 00391-3349
(public)

South Carolina

University of South Carolina
Law School
Maine and Greene Streets
Columbia 29208
(803) 777-6617
(public)

South Dakota

University of South Dakota
School of Law
Vermillion 57069
(605) 677-5443
(public)

Tennessee

Memphis State University
Cecil C. Humphreys School of Law
Memphis 38152
(901) 454-2421
(public)

University of Tennessee
College of Law
1505 West Cumberland Avenue
Knoxville 37996-1800
(615) 974-4241
(public)

Vanderbilt University
School of Law
Nashville 37240
(615) 322-2615
(private)

Texas

Baylor University
School of Law
Waco 76798
(817) 755-1911
(private)

St. Mary's University
School of Law
One Camino Santa Maria
San Antonio 78284
(512) 436-3424
(private)

Southern Methodist University
School of Law
Dallas 75275
(214) 692-2618
(private)

South Texas College of Law
1303 San Jacinto Street
Houston 77002
(713) 659-8040
(private)

Texas Southern University
Thurgood Marshall School of Law
3100 Cleburne Avenue
Houston 77004
(713) 527-7112
(public)

Texas Tech University
School of Law
Lubbock 79409
(806) 742-3791
(public)

University of Houston
Law Center
4800 Calhoun
Houston 77004
(713) 749-1422
(public)

University of Texas
School of Law
727 East 26th Street
Austin 78705
(512) 471-5151
(public)

Utah

Brigham Young University
J. Reuben Clark Law School
Provo 84602
(801) 378-4274
(private)

University of Utah
College of Law
Salt Lake City 84112
(801) 581-6833
(public)

Vermont

Vermont Law School
South Royalton 05608
(802) 763-8303
(private)

Virginia

College of William and Mary
Marshall-Wythe School of Law
Williamsburg 23185
(804) 253-4304
(public)

George Mason University
School of Law
3401 North Fairfax Drive
Arlington 22201
(703) 841-2610
(public)

University of Richmond
T.C. Williams School of Law
Richmond 23173
(804) 285-6336
(private)

University of Virginia
School of Law
Charlottesville 22901
(804) 924-7343
(public)

Washington and Lee University
School of Law
Lewis Hall
Lexington 24450
(703) 463-9111
(private)

Washington

Gonzaga University
School of Law
P.O. Box 3528
Spokane 99220-3528
(509) 328-4220
(private)

University of Puget Sound
School of Law
950 Broadway Plaza
Tacoma 98402
(206) 756-3500
(private)

University of Washington
School of Law
Condon Hall
1100 N.E. Campus Parkway
Seattle 98105
(206) 543-4550
(public)

West Virginia

West Virginia University
College of Law
Law Center
Morgantown 26506
(304) 293-5306
(public)

Wisconsin

Marquette University
Law School
1103 West Wisconsin Avenue
Milwaukee 53233
(414) 224-7090
(private)

University of Wisconsin
Law School
Madison 53706
(608) 262-2240
(public)

Wyoming

University of Wyoming
College of Law
P.O. Box 3035 University Station
Laramie, 82071
(307) 766-6416
(public)

Selected Bibliography

Darrow, Clarence. *The Story of My Life*. New York: Charles Scribner's Sons, 1932.

Dershowitz, Alan M. *The Best Defense*. New York: Random House, 1982.

Freedman, Lawrence Meir. *A History of American Law*. New York: Simon & Schuster, 1973.

Goldfarb, Sally F. *Inside the Law Schools: A Guide by Students, for Students*. New York: E. P. Dutton, 1982.

Mayer, Martin. *The Lawyers*. Westport, Conn.: Greenwood Press, 1980.

Rembar, Charles. *The Law of the Land: The Evolution of Our Legal System*. New York: Simon & Schuster, 1981.

Stewart, James B. *The Partners: Inside America's Most Powerful Law Firms*. New York: Simon & Schuster, 1983.

Turow, Scott. *One L: An Inside Account of Life in the First Year at Harvard Law School*. New York: Penguin Books, 1978.

LSAT Review Books

Bobrow, Jerry. *Baron's Guide to the New Law School Admission Test*. Woodbury, New York: Baron's Educational Series, 1983.

Crocetti, Gino, and B.M. Clarke, JD. *LSAT: Law School Admission Test*. New York: Arco, 1983.

Tajgman, David, JD. *Lovejoy's Preparation for the LSAT*. New York: Monarch Press, 1984.

Volkell, Randolph Z., JD. *LSAT Preparation Guide*. 3rd ed. New York: Wiley Press, 1983.

About the Author

LAWRENCE GRAHAM is currently a student at Harvard Law School and the author of several books including *Conquering College Life* and *Ten Point Plan for College Acceptance.* A 1983 graduate of Princeton University, Graham has worked as student producer with NBC Studios, job and career counselor at Princeton Career Services, research assistant at the Ford Foundation, and aide for the assistant to the President at the White House. His first books brought him nationwide recognition in *The New York Times*, *People Magazine*, *Good Housekeeping*, on the *Phil Donahue Show* and *Today Show* and in other forms of national media. He has counseled and lectured to groups in schools, libraries, and community centers around the country on college- and job-related matters.